ARPEGGIO

FOR THE MODERN GUITARIST

by Stephen Ross

ISBN 978-0-634-08609-0

HAL•LEONARD®
CORPORATION

7777 W. BLUEMOUND RD. P.O. BOX 13819 MILWAUKEE, WI 53213

In Australia Contact:
Hal Leonard Australia Pty. Ltd.
4 Lentara Court
Cheltenham, Victoria, 3192 Australia
Email: ausadmin@halleonard.com.au

Visit Hal Leonard Online at
www.halleonard.com

ACKNOWLEDGMENTS

I would like to thank everyone at Hal Leonard for making this book happen. I also want to thank Andy Martin, for contacts and advice, and Ron Cannella, for too many things to list.

Thanks also go to the following people for inspiration and support: Aunt Anne, Uncle Charlie, Laura and Charlie, Carol and Chris, Billy, Dianne and Mark, Alicia, Kevin, Max, Charlotte, Jackson, Uncle Eddie and Aunt Josephine, Grandma and Grandpa Figler, Grandma and Grandpa Rogouski, Jacqueline Bittner, Chris Harding, Stevie Ray Vaughan, Jimi Hendrix, Jackie Gleason, Art Carney, Audrey Meadows, Joyce Randoff, Carole King, John Muire, all of my past and present students for keeping me on my toes, all of the musicians I have played with over the years, Ibanez, Ovation, Carvin, Mesa Boogie, Gibson, Fender, Line 6, Steinberg, Yahama, Music Man, Marshall, DBX, *Guitar Player*, *Guitar World*, *Guitar* One, Simon Batham and Amir Shmuell, Rusty Cooley, Joy Basu, Richie Kotzen, Jarrett Dean, Rich Dunn, Glenn Acker, Rich Mattalian, Steve D'Acutas at Soundspa, Dale Toth, Larry and Leslie, Hal Seltzer, D'Addario, and all other friends and acquaintances I may have forgotten.

Very special thanks to Mom, Dad, and brother Stan for their love and support, my soulmate and love Adriana Fitzsimmons and God for keeping me on the right path.

TABLE OF CONTENTS

ABOUT THE AUTHOR

Stephen Rogouski (aka Stephen Ross) has been a professional guitarist for eighteen years. His most recent project, Rogosonic, has released a new CD called *Leave the World Alone*. Additionally, he has released a solo album titled *Midnight Drive* on the highly acclaimed Shrapnel label, appeared on numerous other notable recordings such as *Warmth in the Wilderness, Part II* (Lion Music) and *The Alchemist* (Liquid Note Records), received praise from several major guitar publications, and contributed guitar lessons to several online instructional web sites. He currently lives in Monmouth Junction, New Jersey. To contact Stephen, or to order *Leave the World Alone*, visit him at stephenross.com.

PREFACE

My first real jazz teacher was Harry Leahey, who not only was a student of the great Johnny Smith but also toured with Phil Woods and taught at William Paterson College. He was a legend in the area, and almost every guitarist worth his or her salt studied with him at one time or another. I recall that my mom would drive me to his large Victorian house in South Plainfield, New Jersey, for my lessons, and we would wait in a small room with food and cigarette ashes strewn about while he finished his previous student's lesson. As we sat waiting, the sound of wonderful bebop licks would emerge from the teaching room. Usually it would take about ten minutes before the door would spring open and a smiling Harry would greet us and call me in.

It was in those lessons with Harry that I was first introduced to arpeggios and chord theory. I have always loved the sound of arpeggios and feel they are an important part of my guitar style. Thus I felt compelled to share my insights and ideas by writing this book. I hope you enjoy learning from it as much as I enjoyed writing it.

If you have any questions regarding this book, please visit www.arpeggiosforthemodernguitarist.com. This website will also include errata, upcoming events and appearances, and a monthly blog and forum.

INTRODUCTION

Why this book?

OK, so here's another book on arpeggios. What makes this one different from the others? Most arpeggio books I have seen focus primarily on forms with little information on how to play them effectively. In this book, the forms given are designed around certain techniques such as sweep picking, alternate picking, legato playing, two-hand tapping, and multi-finger tapping. If you can play one form well using one particular technique, you should not have too much trouble playing the other forms well using that same technique.

Prerequisites

Many musicians think of arpeggios as an intermediate to advanced topic—and they're right! To use this book effectively, you should understand what scales and modes are, know how to play and transpose them in different keys, understand basic chord theory, and have some knowledge of meter and rhythm.

Methodology

An arpeggio book must teach the student arpeggio forms and show how to execute and apply them. The challenge in creating a successful text is carefully blending and balancing these topics.

1. **Learning arpeggio forms:** To learn arpeggio forms effectively, they must be organized in a structured and logical manner. This book organizes arpeggios by tonality and harmonic complexity. The tonality of the arpeggio is simply designated as major, dominant, minor, diminished, or augmented. Harmonic complexity is closely related to the number of notes in the chord formula; for example, a Gmaj13 arpeggio is considered more harmonically complex than a G major.

   To make memorizing arpeggio forms easier, forms that are harmonically complex are sometimes built by stacking basic forms; for example, seventh arpeggios, which have four-note chord formulas, can be built by stacking three-note triad forms. This approach is utilized quite frequently throughout the text.

2. **Playing arpeggio forms:** This book integrates practice tips and execution notes throughout each chapter. Techniques covered in this book include alternate picking, sweep picking, hammer-ons and pull-offs, two-hand tapping, and string skipping.

3. **Application:** Integrating arpeggios into your playing style is the part of the process that takes the longest amount of time, but is also the most rewarding. By the time you are finished with this book, you should be well on your way to integrating the arpeggio forms illustrated in this book as well as your own into your playing style.

HOW TO PRACTICE ARPEGGIOS

It is important to practice frequently, but it's more important to make sure you are getting the most out of your practice sessions. Here are the seven golden rules of practicing arpeggios. Use them wisely.

1. Always use a metronome

I cannot stress enough the importance of using a metronome. It's the only way to develop timing and groove, two essential ingredients in any style of music. The standard approach is to start at a slow tempo and gradually increase it as you perfect each speed. Here are some additional tips to flesh that out a bit.

Establish a pulse on the metronome and then play through different note groupings, such as quarter notes, quarter-note triplets, eighth notes, eighth-note triplets, sixteenth notes, and sixteenth-note triplets. After exhausting all of the possibilities at one tempo, increase the tempo and repeat the procedure. Another way to look at this is to play one note per beat, two notes per beat, three notes per beat, and so on, until you reach your maximum speed.

It is also important to be able to start your phrase on any part of the beat. When playing eighth notes, practice starting on the upbeat. When playing sixteenth notes, practice starting your phrases on each of the four subdivisions. Use the same approach on triplets and their subdivisions.

Another very useful way to practice with a metronome is to go back and forth between rhythm and lead playing. This forces you to adapt new arpeggio runs in a variety of timing situations. Many times you will have to end the arpeggio phrase in different spots to keep the groove going. A solo can get boring real fast if arpeggios always start and end on the root. You want to be able to start and end them on any note of the arpeggio.

2. Play arpeggios in all twelve keys

See Chapter 8 (Key Transposition)

3. Establish reference points

It is much easier to learn new arpeggio forms when you associate them with chord shapes or scale patterns that you already know. For example, here is a G major arpeggio based on the 6th-string root G barre chord, and a C major arpeggio based on the 5th-string root C barre chord.

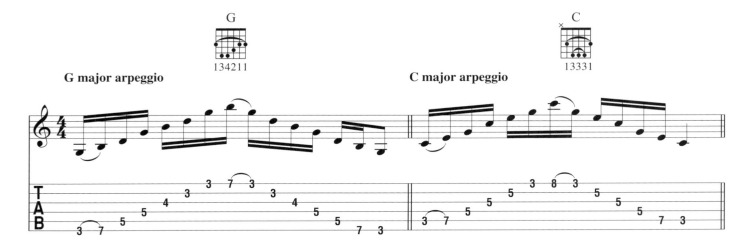

You can establish this kind of reference point with any chord shape and quality (Gm, G7, etc.). Start with the 6th- and 5th-string rooted barre chords of the most common chord qualities. Then establish the same types of reference points with various scale shapes. For example, here are G minor and C minor arpeggio shapes based on their respective minor pentatonic scale shapes.

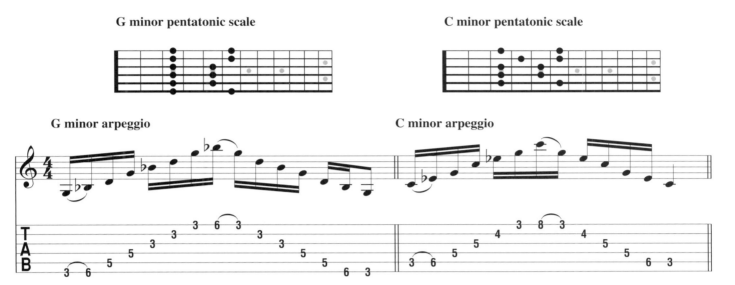

4. Connect forms together in creative ways

The ability to move around the neck fluently through all of the arpeggio forms provides greater creative freedom and leads to more interesting lines. To begin developing this skill, first select several *target arpeggios* that you would like to connect together, say, in three different neck positions. The next step is to connect them together in one line. The only requirement should be that at least part of each target arpeggio should be included in the line. Everything else such as how you connect the arpeggios, what techniques are used, whether or not chromatic tones or scales tones are included in the line is left up the individual.

Here is an example connecting a Gmaj9 with a Gmaj7 octave arpeggio, both in root position.

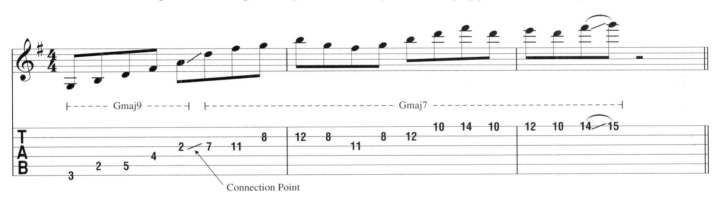

Here is a slightly more involved example, comprising three inversions of a Gmaj7 arpeggio.

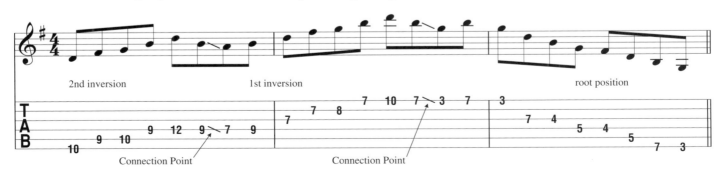

7

Another way to practice connecting arpeggios is to outline a chord progression such as this I–IV–V–I in the key of C major (C–F–G–C).

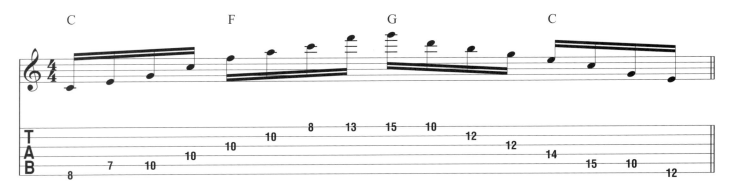

As you practice making these connections, be sure to vary the rhythms, note durations, and note groupings in your arpeggio runs.

5. Practice arpeggios using different patterns

Here is a good routine for practicing patterns. First, choose an arpeggio form. For this example, we will use a G major 1st inversion major triad arpeggio. Then apply these two-note, three-note, and four-note patterns:

Two-note patterns

Three-note patterns

Four-note patterns

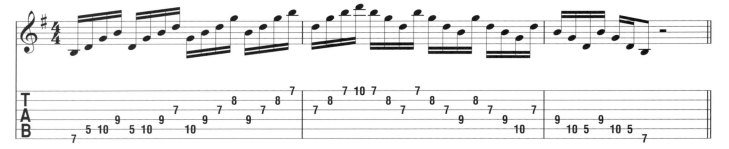

As you work through the arpeggio forms in this book, try applying these three patterns to each one. Once you can do that smoothly and fluidly, you will be well on your way to mastering the forms.

6. Play over rhythm tracks

Practicing arpeggios by themselves can lead to sounding like you're simply playing finger exercises. To develop more musical applications of these arpeggios, record some common chord progression such as I–IV–V or I–ii–VI–V in all 12 keys and improvise guitar solos over them using your new arpeggio forms. Try to translate the musical ideas in your head to the guitar. The focus here should be making music out of the arpeggios.

7. Sing the notes of the arpeggios

Even if you cannot sing very well, try doing this. It is very good for helping you hear melodies and ideas in your head. If you can hear good ideas in your head, you need to be able to translate them to the guitar, and the only way to accomplish that is with practice. This is the key to forming your own style and being true to your inner musical voice.

SWEEP PICKING

An important technique for playing arpeggios is *sweep picking*. In executing this technique, you'll push (ascending) and drag (descending) your pick across the strings, rather than using a conventional alternate-picking approach. You will find that extraneous noise is an issue when using the sweep picking technique. To minimize this, use a slight palm mute with your picking hand in conjunction with releasing fret-hand pressure immediately after a note has been struck. Make sure that the notes of the arpeggio do not blend into each other. To help get you ready to play the rest of the arpeggio forms in this book, here are some good sweep-picking exercises.

To get comfortable with the sweeping motion, take a chord form such as this root-position G major barre chord and practice sweeping up and down the chord.

G major arpeggio

Once you're comfortable with the sweeping motion, the next step is to synchronize the fret hand. Practice this exercise by lifting up each finger of the left hand after striking the note. This will give the arpeggio a nice tight sound.

TRACK 1 · 0:00 FAST/SLOW

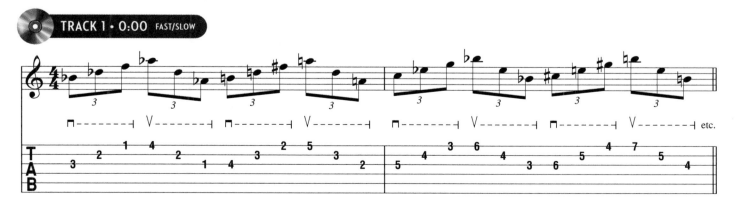

Next, try a more complex example that involves a fret-hand position shift in the middle of the arpeggio form (here, the shift occurs between strings 4 and 3), like this tritone-based exercise.

 TRACK 1 • 0:18

The final step in sweep picking is being able to incorporate hammer-ons and pull-offs into the sweeping motion. This exercise will help develop that technique.

TRACK 1 • 0:28 FAST/SLOW

CHAPTER 1
TRIAD ARPEGGIOS

The most logical starting place when it comes to mastering arpeggios is the triad, which serves as the foundation for more complex arpeggios like the ones you'll learn in later chapters. Triads contain three notes, which are typically repeated in other octaves when playing arpeggios. There are four basic triad tonalities: major, minor, diminished, and augmented. We define the triad tonality as it relates to the major scale, using a specific chord formula to build the arpeggio. The major scale contains seven notes, or scale degrees, which for the purpose of constructing chords and arpeggios are labeled with the numerals 1–7. Below are the chord formulas for the triad arpeggios we will cover in this section, with each numeral representing the appropriate scale degree from the major scale.

All of the arpeggio forms that follow in this chapter will be presented using the note G as the root. Since we are using G as our root, we can use the chord formulas above to spell out the notes of each triad arpeggio for each different tonality, as shown here.

To facilitate the learning process, I will break the arpeggios into several smaller pieces, demonstrating one-, two-, three-, four-, five-, and six-string forms.

ONE-STRING TRIAD ARPEGGIOS

You may be asking yourself, "Is it really worth learning arpeggios on just one string?" And the answer is: "Yes, it is!" Learning arpeggios on one string not only helps you understand the intervallic relationships between the notes of each arpeggio but also helps you get a more complete picture of the guitar neck, which in turn will make connecting them easier.

Here are the major, minor, diminished, and augmented one-string arpeggio forms as found on the first string, using a G root note.

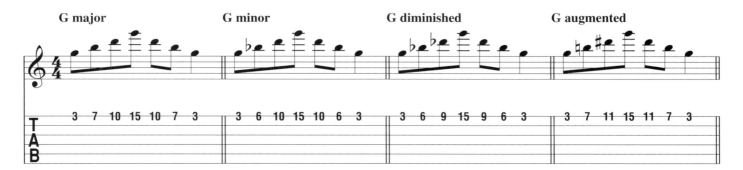

Practice each of these forms in all twelve keys.

TWO-STRING TRIAD ARPEGGIOS

Adding the second string to the mix makes it easy to see that each arpeggio form within a certain tonality (i.e., major, minor) has a different starting note. When an arpeggio starts on a note other than the root, it is called an *inversion*. Since a triad has three different notes, it can also have three different inversions. The starting note in the arpeggio determines the inversion. In G, if the arpeggio starts on the root, it is called the *root position* arpeggio; if it starts on B (3rd), it is called a *first inversion* arpeggio; and if it starts on D (5th), it is called a *second inversion* arpeggio.

Here are the three shapes for each form, in major, minor, diminished, and augmented tonalities.

Major

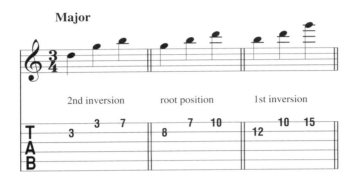

Minor

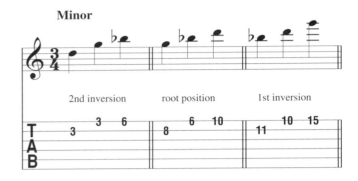

Diminished

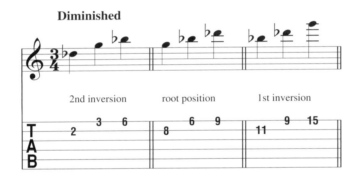

Augmented

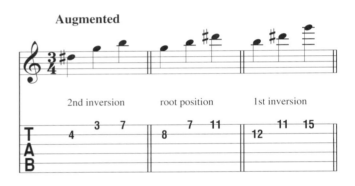

PRACTICE NOTES:

Use sweep picking to play these two-string triad arpeggios. Play each one twice, with a triplet feel (sextuplets) before moving up to the next inversion. This is demonstrated below on the major form. Do the same exercise on all other forms (minor, diminished, and augmented).

TRACK 2

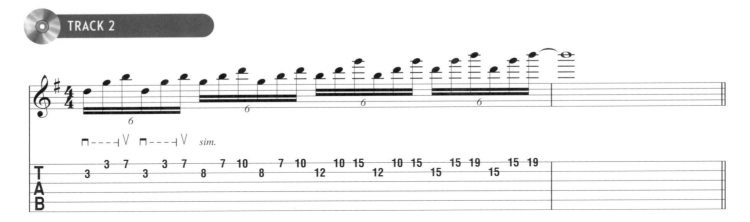

THREE-STRING TRIAD ARPEGGIOS

If you've memorized the two-string arpeggios, the three-string versions will come easy, as they use the same shape, only with an added note on the third string.

Major

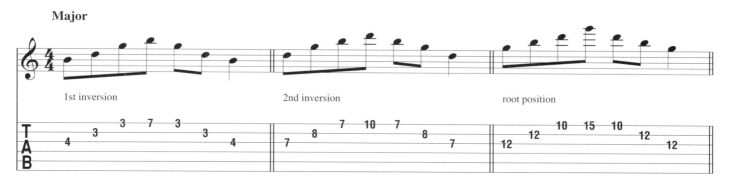

Minor

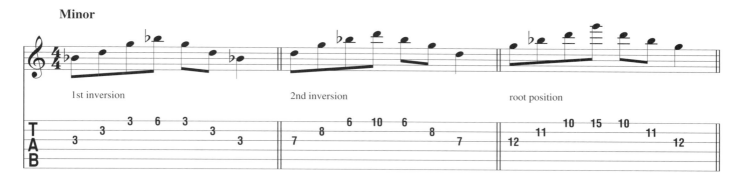

Diminished

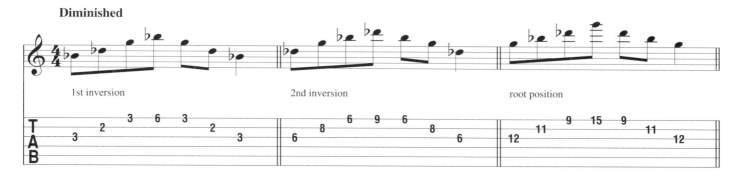

Augmented

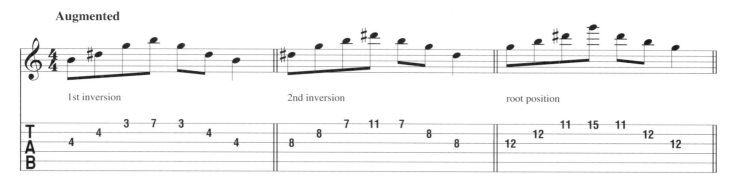

> **PRACTICE NOTES:**
> Unlike the two-string sweeps, these three-string shapes require both downward and upward sweeps. Additionally, you'll need to add pull-offs to your sweep picking technique. Try to use economy of motion, keeping your fret hand's fingers as close to the neck as possible.

The following example connects the major inversions together by shifting positions with the pinky. It should also be practiced on minor and augmented forms.

FOUR-, FIVE-, AND SIX-STRING TRIAD ARPEGGIOS

Below you will find the six-string forms of major, minor, diminished, and augmented triad arpeggios, with a G root. To get the five-string forms, just leave out the note on the sixth string, and to get the four-string forms, leave out the notes on the sixth and fifth strings.

Major

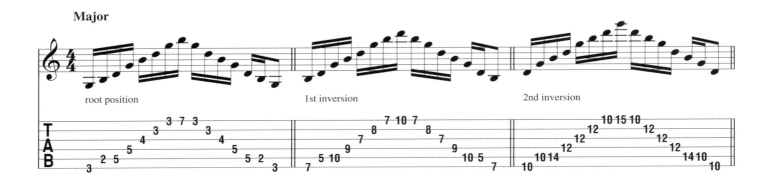

Minor

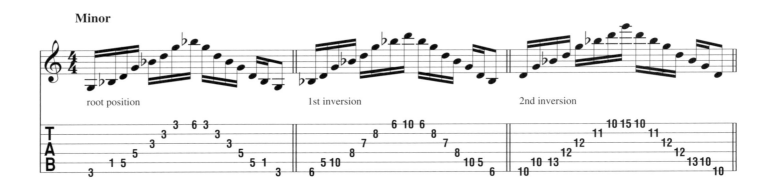

Diminished

root position   1st inversion   2nd inversion

Augmented

root position   1st inversion   2nd inversion

PRACTICE NOTES:

Sweeping the four-, five-, and six-string forms will take a bit more practice than the previous forms. The example below demonstrates the technique using a five-string form. To execute these sweeps effectively, you'll need to be comfortable hammering onto a note during the ascending part of the sweep and then pulling off during the descent. An alternative way to execute these is to alternate pick both notes on the high E string, rather than using the pull-off.

When you get to the second arpeggio form (beat 2), try to keep your second finger planted on the B string when sweeping across the G, B, and E strings. The example below ascends one form, then shifts up to the next form with the pinky and descends. It is shown below using the major inversions and played as sextuplets. Be sure to adapt this exercise to the minor, diminished, and augmented forms as well.

TRACK 4 FAST/SLOW

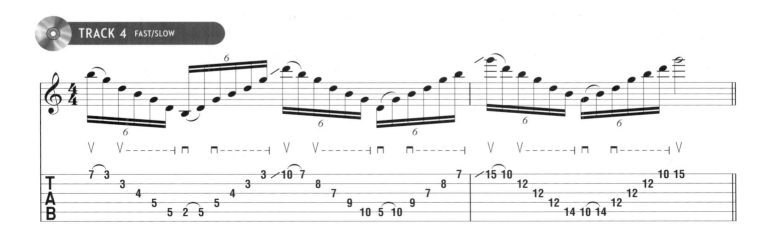

CHAPTER 2
SEVENTH CHORD ARPEGGIOS

Now that you've got a good grasp on triad arpeggios, let's take the next step and add the seventh scale degree to the triad forms, to create more complex and colorful sounds. Shown here are the chord formulas for the most common seventh-chord forms.

Having a solid understanding of these chord formulas will be very useful when learning new arpeggio forms. For instance, once you've got a major seventh form under your fingers, you can find the dominant seventh form simply by lowering the seventh degree by one half step, or by one fret. This idea of *referential forms* can be applied to all of the different arpeggio inversions.

DIMINISHED SEVENTH ARPEGGIO

This is a rather unique arpeggio, since one form covers all keys. Because there are no perfect intervals in this form, the notes repeat every minor 3rd interval. For example, the notes of a G°7 arpeggio are G–B♭–D♭–F♭. Going up a minor 3rd, to B♭°7, the notes are B♭–D♭–F♭–A♭♭ (enharmonically, G). They contain the same notes. This means there are only three distinct diminished seventh arpeggios: G, A♭, and A. Here is a summary of the equivalent diminished seventh arpeggios.

$$G°7 = B♭°7 = D♭°7 = E°7$$

$$A♭°7 = B°7 = D°7 = F°7$$

$$A°7 = C°7 = E♭°7 = G♭°7$$

BUILDING ON PREVIOUS KNOWLEDGE

Here is another interesting idea you can use when constructing seventh arpeggios, to make learning new forms easier. Up to this point, you should have memorized the triad arpeggios in major, minor, diminished, and augmented forms. So wouldn't it be nice to be able to use these familiar triad forms to construct seventh arpeggios? Well, you can, using an approach called triad stacking. The technique involves stacking two triads that, when combined, provide all four notes of a particular seventh chord. The utility of *triad stacking* is especially evident on the forms that use more than three strings.

Here's how it works: To build a major seventh arpeggio, take your designated root note and add the minor triad that occurs a 3rd above the root. For example, to create a Gmaj7 arpeggio (G–B–D–F♯), start with the root major triad, G (G–B–D), and then add the minor triad a 3rd above G—in this case, Bm (B–D–F♯). Put those two together, and it's easy to see that adding a B minor triad to the G produces the Gmaj7. Even without the G, playing a B minor triad over a G major chord will yield the same effect.

Here is a breakdown of the triad stacking principle as it is used in constructing many of the arpeggio forms in this chapter.

TARGET	STACKED TRIADS	
SEVENTH ARPEGGIOS	TRIAD 1	TRIAD 2
Gmaj7	G major (G–B–D)	B minor (B–D–F♯)
G7	G major (G–B–D)	B diminished (B–D–F)
Gm7	G minor (G–B♭–D)	B♭ major (B♭–D–F)
G°7	G diminished (G–B♭–D♭)	B♭ diminished (B♭–D♭–F♭)

ONE-STRING SEVENTH ARPEGGIOS

OK, let's start learning some of these seventh-chord arpeggio forms. As in the previous chapter, all of the arpeggio forms here will be created from a G root, but should be learned and practiced in all keys.

One-string Major Seventh Arpeggios

As with the triad arpeggio forms, we'll begin with single-string shapes, to aid in future fretboard navigation. Here, the Gmaj7 arpeggio is attained simply by adding an F♯ to the G major triad form from the previous chapter.

TRACK 5 · 0:00

One-string Dominant Seventh Arpeggios

To create the dominant seventh arpeggio, start with the major seventh form above, and lower the 7th by one fret (F♯ to F).

TRACK 5 · 0:06

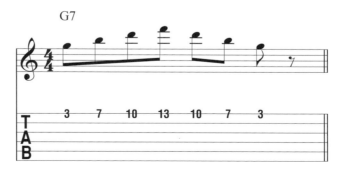

One-string Minor Seventh Arpeggios

Here, start with the dominant seventh form and lower the 3rd by one fret (B to B♭).

 **TRACK 5 · 0:12**

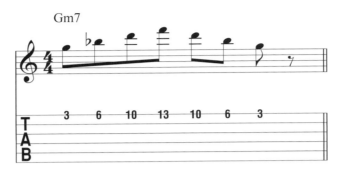

One-string Minor Seventh, Flat Fifth Arpeggios

To make the minor-seventh-flat-fifth arpeggio, begin with the minor seventh form and lower the 5th by a half step, or one fret.

 **TRACK 5 · 0:18**

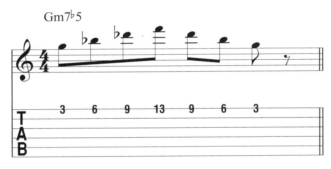

One-string Diminished Seventh Arpeggios

Here, take the minor-seventh-flat-fifth form above, and lower the 7th by another half step. With reference to the original major seventh form, the 7th degree is now *double flatted*. A double-flatted 7th is enharmonically the same as a major 6th, which is how diminished chords are often spelled, for ease of reading. For example, here, F♭ is notated simply as E.

 **TRACK 5 · 0:24**

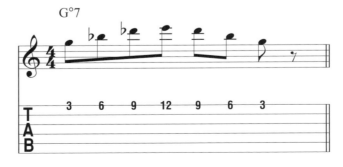

TWO-STRING SEVENTH ARPEGGIOS

As we look at two-string forms (and more), inversions once again come into play. Because seventh chords contain four notes, there are now three inversions possible in addition to the root-position form. For demonstration purposes, we'll show each form starting in the lowest possible fretboard location, regardless of inversion.

> **NOTE:**
>
> These two-string forms will be very useful when the concept of octave arpeggios is introduced in Chapter 5.

Two-string Major Seventh Arpeggios

TRACK 6

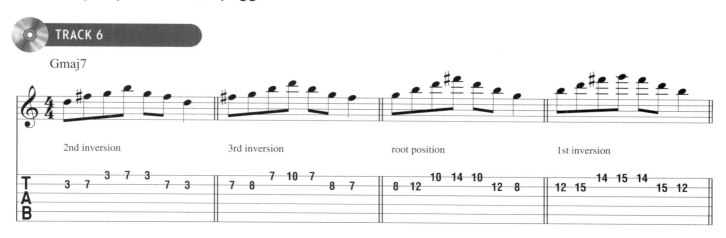

Two-string Dominant Seventh Arpeggios

TRACK 7

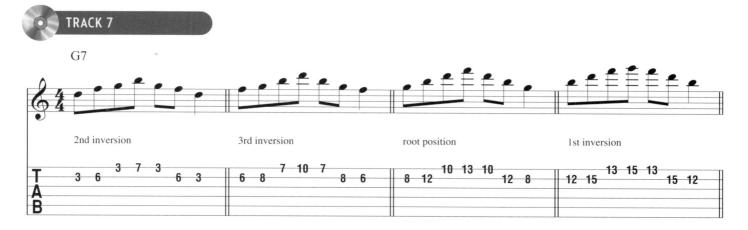

Two-string Minor Seventh Arpeggios

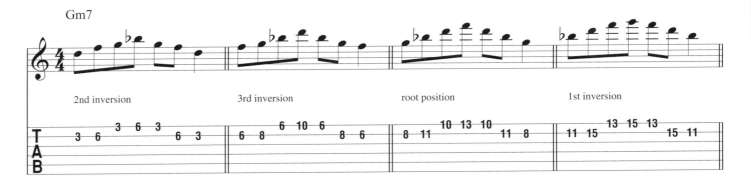

Gm7

2nd inversion   3rd inversion   root position   1st inversion

Two-string Minor Seventh, Flat Fifth Arpeggios

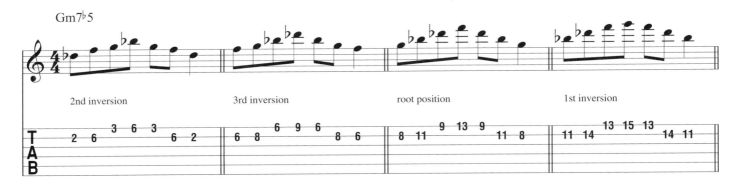

Gm7♭5

2nd inversion   3rd inversion   root position   1st inversion

Two-string Diminished Seventh Arpeggios

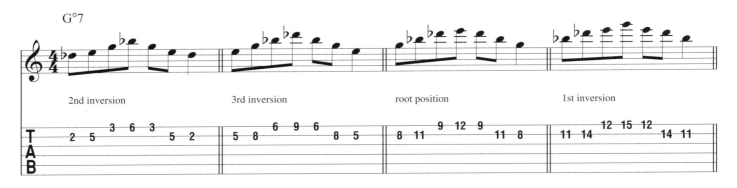

G°7

2nd inversion   3rd inversion   root position   1st inversion

As you practice the preceding two-string shapes, you should play them with two different approaches. First, you can alternate pick every note, starting on an upstroke. Second, use hammer-ons and pull-offs as shown here.

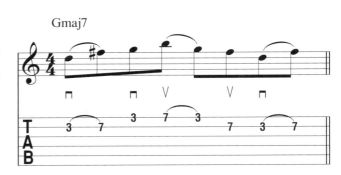

Gmaj7

THREE-STRING SEVENTH ARPEGGIOS

Now it's time to add a third string to the seventh-chord arpeggio forms. As you play through these forms, you'll notice that some work best with sweep picking, and some with alternate picking. I suggest using sweep picking whenever possible.

Three-string Major Seventh Arpeggios

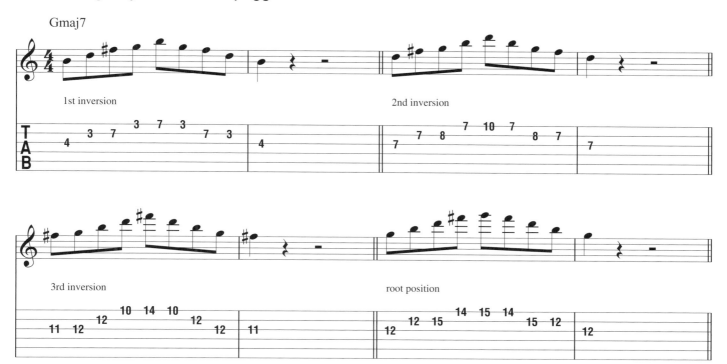

Three-string Dominant Seventh Arpeggios

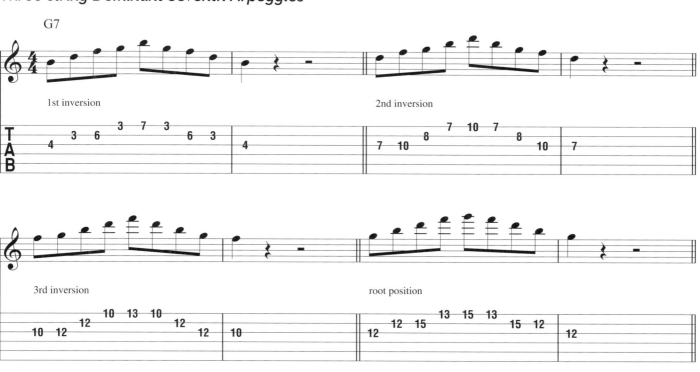

Three-string Minor Seventh Arpeggios

Three-string Minor Seventh, Flat Fifth Arpeggios

Three-string Diminished Seventh Arpeggios

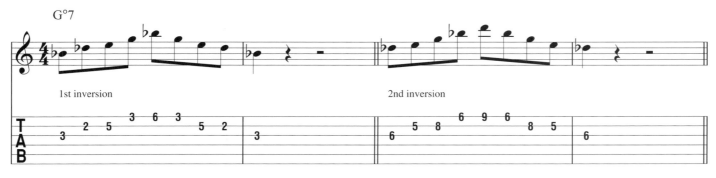

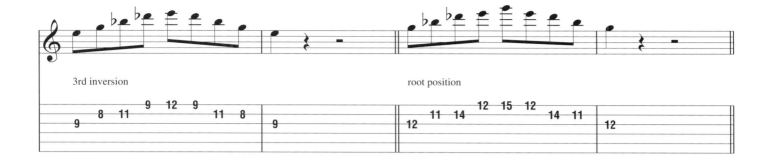

FOUR-, FIVE-, AND SIX-STRING SEVENTH ARPEGGIOS

To make these forms more finger-friendly, I took the liberty of leaving out certain notes in the arpeggio that make the patterns hard to play; for example, in the root-position Gmaj7 form, I leave out the G root note on the D string, at the fifth fret. Coincidentally, this provides a great example of the utility of the stacked triads approach, as the Gmaj7 form is essentially a B minor triad form stuffed between bookend G notes.

As with the triad arpeggio forms in the previous chapter, only six-string seventh-chord arpeggio forms are presented here. Be sure to practice the four- and five-string forms as well, eliminating the low A and E strings as necessary.

Six-string Major Seventh Arpeggios

Six-string Dominant Seventh Arpeggios

Using the previous major seventh forms as a reference, find all of the F♯ notes and flat them to get these dominant forms. These fingerings are not as easy to play as the major seventh ones, but they are still manageable.

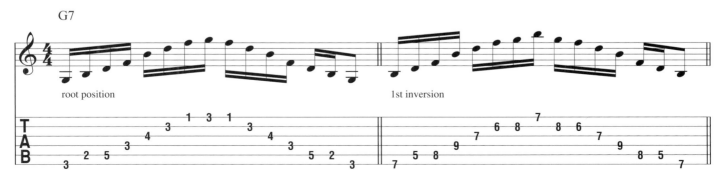

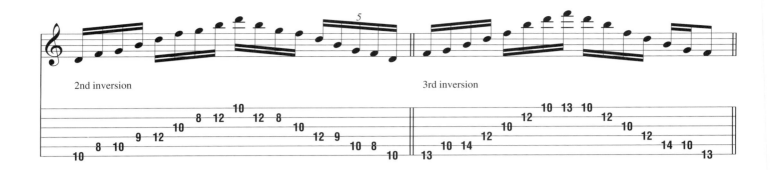

Six-string Minor Seventh Arpeggios

You may find your knowledge of triad arpeggio forms useful for navigating these examples. Notice that the root-position Gm7 form is a B♭ major triad arpeggio with an added G note on the sixth and first strings. All of these shapes are very similar to the B♭ major triad form, with only slight variations.

Six-string Minor Seventh, Flat Fifth Arpeggios

Again, your knowledge of triad forms will come in handy. Here, if a G note is added to a B♭ minor triad, you get the target Gm7♭5 form.

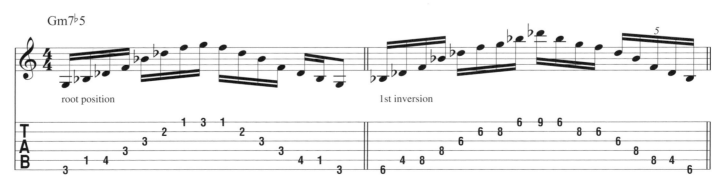

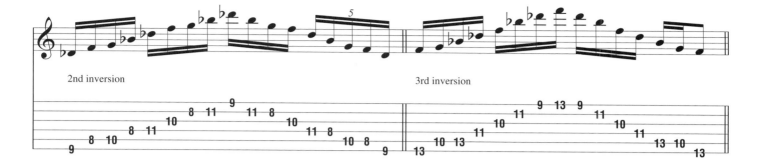

2nd inversion   *3rd inversion*

Six-string Diminished Seventh Arpeggios

The same form is used for all inversions and all keys.

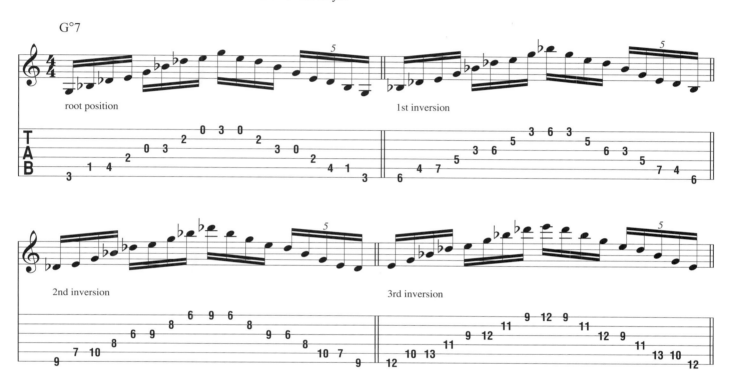

All of these four-, five-, and six-string forms are designed specifically for sweep picking. During the ascending part of the arpeggios, all notes are played with either a hammer-on or a down-sweep (any necessary hammer-ons should be executed during the down-sweep). During the descending part of the arpeggio, all notes are played with either an up-sweep or a pull-off (any pull-offs should be executed during the up-sweep).

The technique is demonstrated below with the root position six-string Gmaj7 arpeggio form.

TRACK 8   FAST/SLOW

CHAPTER 3
EXTENDED CHORDS (9THS, 11THS, AND 13THS)

More color can be added to arpeggios by adding extensions such as 9ths, 11ths, and 13ths. These extended forms lead to some really interesting sounds and can add a new dimension to a rock guitar solo. Most of the forms in this chapter can be produced by triad stacking as explained in Chapter 2, or by adding an extra note to a triad arpeggio. The key is to utilize information that has already been learned.

Here is a breakdown of the triad stacking principle used in constructing many of the arpeggio forms that follow.

TARGET	STACKED TRIADS	
NINTH ARPEGGIO	TRIAD 1	TRIAD 2
Maj9 (1–3–5–7–9)	I major	V major
Dom9 (1–3–5–♭7–9)	I major	V minor
Min9 (1–♭3–5–♭7–9)	I minor	V minor

TARGET	STACKED TRIADS		
ELEVENTH ARPEGGIO	TRIAD 1	TRIAD 2	TRIAD 3
Maj11 (1–3–5–7–9–11)	I major	VII diminished	V major
Dom11 (1–3–5–♭7–9–11)	I major	♭VII major	V minor
Min11 (1–♭3–5–♭7–9–11)	I minor	♭VII major	V minor

TARGET	STACKED TRIADS		
THIRTEENTH ARPEGGIO	TRIAD 1	TRIAD 2	TRIAD 3
Maj13 (1–3–5–7–9–11–13)	I major	VI minor	III minor
Dom13 (1–3–5–♭7–9–11–13)	I major	VI minor	V minor
Min13 (1–♭3–5–♭7–9–11–13)	I minor	VI diminished	V minor

All of the arpeggio forms that follow will contain a G root note. Be sure to play these forms in all keys.

NINTH ARPEGGIOS

Major Ninth Arpeggios

Superimposing triad arpeggios is a great way to create major ninth forms. Here are the steps involved in creating a Gmaj9 arpeggio using triad forms we have already learned. The first step is to look at the formula for the Gmaj9 arpeggio: 1–3–5–7–9 (G–B–D–F#–A). The second step is to find a triad arpeggio in the key of G that will contain extended tones of a Gmaj9 arpeggio. There are seven possible choices, but the G major triad can be ruled out since this would simply be a G major triad arpeggio. That leaves the C, D, Am, Bm, Em, and F#° triad arpeggios.

After analyzing each triad arpeggio over a G root, it can be determined that D major is the triad arpeggio that best creates the Gmaj9 sound when played over a G root. The notes of a D major triad arpeggio are D–F#–A, which are the 5th, 7th, and 9th, respectively, of a Gmaj9 arpeggio. The only note that is missing from the formula is B, the 3rd, which should also be added.

From this analysis, you can conclude that playing a D major triad arpeggio over a Gmaj7 chord will produce a Gmaj9 sound. The beauty of this idea is that new sounds can be produced without having to learn new forms; in this case the D major triad arpeggio, over a chord with a different root, in this case the Gmaj7. Of course, if there is no rhythm guitarist or keyboardist playing the Gmaj7 chord, you'll have to make a few minor adjustments to the D major triad arpeggio. Here are the forms with those slight adjustments.

EXECUTION NOTE:

If there are two notes on a string, the first note is picked and the second is either hammered-on, if ascending, or pulled-off, if descending.

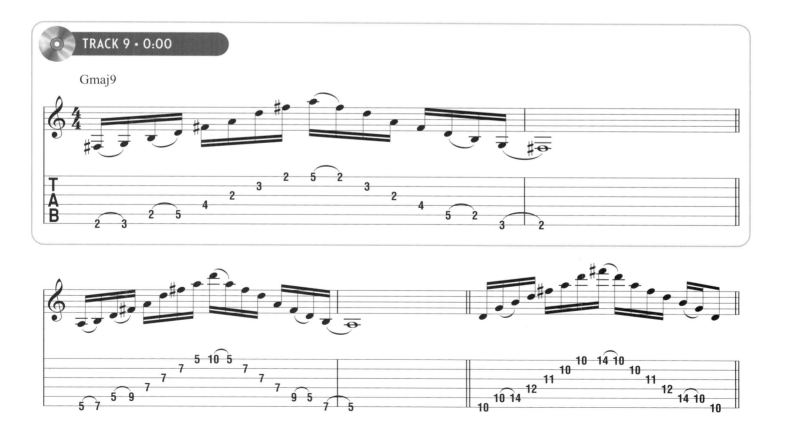

27

Dominant Ninth Arpeggios

Dominant ninth arpeggios can be created in the same way as the major ninth forms. Instead of using a G major scale as our key, however, we use C major, since G7 is in the key of C, not G. In the key of C major, the triad arpeggios are, Dm, Em, Am, C, F, G, and B°. Again, there are seven possible choices, but the G major triad can be ruled out quickly since this would simply be a G major triad arpeggio and does not include any of the extended tones (7ths or 9ths).

After analyzing each of the remaining triad arpeggio over a G root, it can be determined that D minor is the triad arpeggio that best creates the G9 sound when played over a G root. The notes of a D minor triad arpeggio are D–F–A, which are the 5th, ♭7th, and 9th of G9. The only note that is missing from the formula is B, the 3rd, which should also be added.

Notice that when the formula was used to verify the notes of a G9 chord, the G major scale was used instead of C major. That is because the chord formulas have no relationship to keys, only root notes.

Minor Ninth Arpeggios

As with the major and dominant ninth forms, we'll use triad stacking to create our minor ninth forms. Using G as our root, we first need to identify the appropriate scale from which to build our triads. Since Gm9 derives from the G Dorian mode, we'll use the triads diatonic to the key of F: F, Gm, Am, B♭, C, Dm, and E°.

After dispatching the Gm triad and analyzing each remaining one over a G root, it can be determined that D minor is the triad arpeggio that best creates the Gm9 sound when played over a G root. The notes of a D minor triad arpeggio are D–F–A, which are the 5th, ♭7th, and 9th, respectively, of Gm9. To get the minor tonality, however, you must also include the ♭3rd, or B♭.

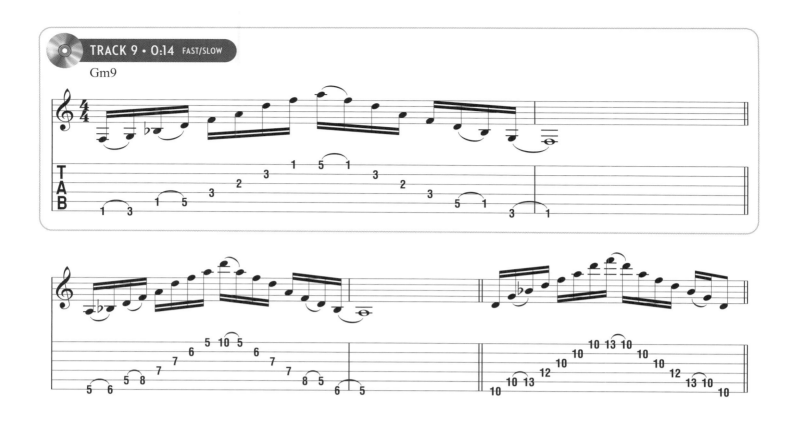

ELEVENTH ARPEGGIOS

Major Eleventh Arpeggios

The chord formula for a major eleventh arpeggio is 1–3–5–7–9–11. To create a Gmaj11 arpeggio, we stack G, F#°, and D triads on top of each other. This stacking process is particularly obvious in the root position form.

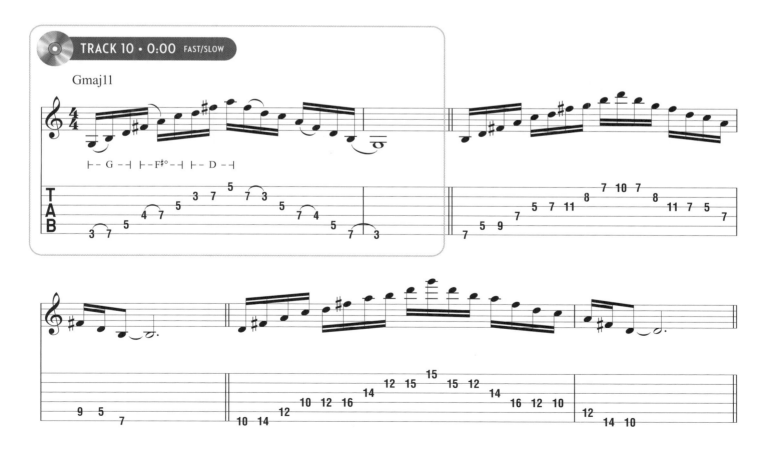

Dominant Eleventh Arpeggios

The chord formula for a dominant eleventh arpeggio is 1–3–5–♭7–9–11. To create a G11 arpeggio, we stack G and F triad arpeggios. You can also add a D minor arpeggio to the stack, but since it contributes only the nonessential 5th to the arpeggio, it is omitted in the following forms.

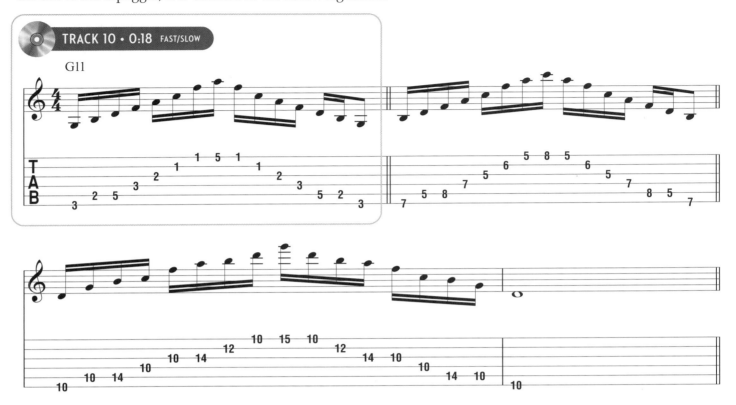

Minor Eleventh Arpeggios

The chord formula for the minor eleventh arpeggio is 1–♭3–5–♭7–9–11. To create a Gm11 arpeggio, we stack Gm and F triad arpeggios. As with the dominant eleventh forms, you can also add a D minor arpeggio, but again, because it contributes only a nonessential 5th, it's omitted from the following forms.

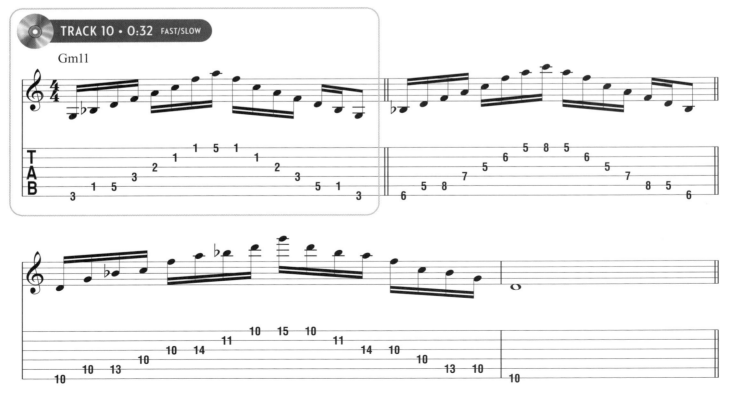

THIRTEENTH ARPEGGIOS

Major Thirteenth Arpeggios

The chord formula for a major thirteenth arpeggio is 1–3–5–7–9–11–13. Although the 11th is *technically* part of the formula, it is typically omitted, and in fact is not included in any of the forms shown below.

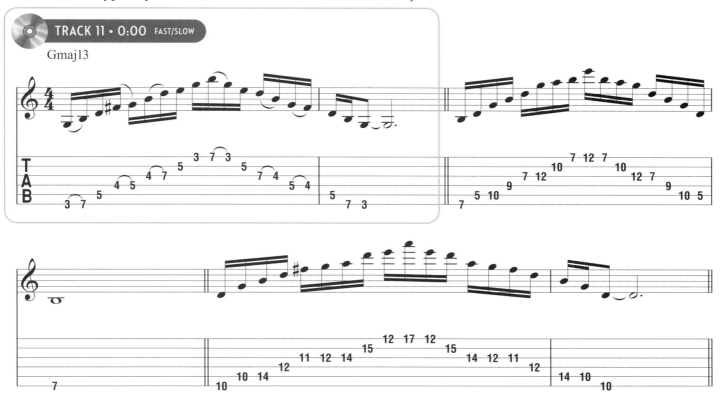

Dominant Thirteenth Arpeggios

The dominant thirteenth chord differs from the major thirteenth chord only in its flatted 7th degree.

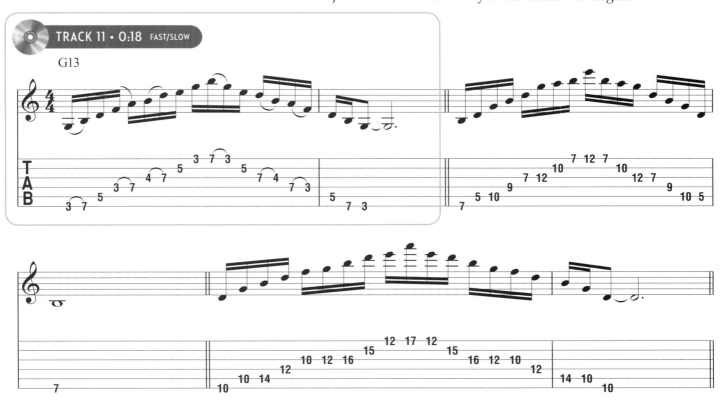

Minor Thirteenth Arpeggios

Note that the following root-position minor thirteenth form contains three notes on the D string, both ascending and descending. To best execute this move, on the ascent strike the first note with your pick, then slide your index finger up two frets and follow with a hammer-on to play the eighth-fret Bb note. On the descent, strike the Bb with your pick, then slide your pinky back to the fifth fret and pull off to the third-fret F note.

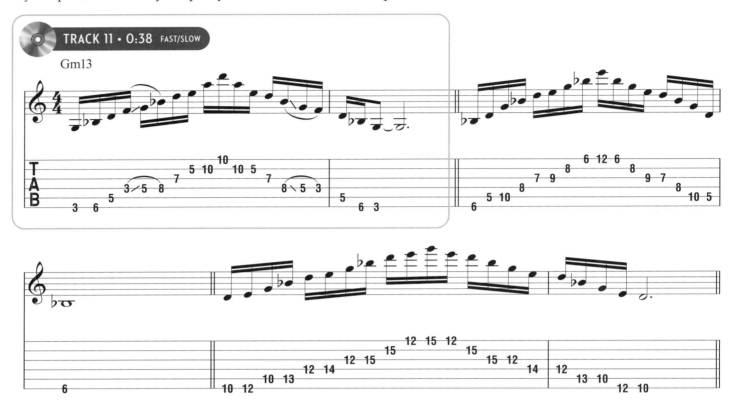

TRACK 11 • 0:38 FAST/SLOW

Gm13

CHAPTER 4
ALTERED DOMINANT ARPEGGIOS

You can add even more color and character to dominant arpeggios by sharping or flatting specific tones, to create *altered dominant* arpeggios. For example, you can create harmonic tension by playing a G7♯5 arpeggio over a G7 chord. To create a G7♯5 arpeggio, simply raise the 5th degree, D, to D♯, resulting in the chord tones G–B–D♯–F. Alternatively, you could also flat the 5th, to D♭, for a G7♭5 arpeggio (G–B–D♭–F).

Shown here is a breakdown of all the altered dominant arpeggios covered in this section, using G as the root.

ARPEGGIO	FORMULA	NOTES
G7♯5	1-3-♯5-♭7	G-B-D♯-F
G7♭5	1-3-♭5-♭7	G-B-D♭-F
G7♯9	1-3-5-♭7-♯9	G-B-D-F-A♯
G7♭9	1-3-5-♭7-♭9	G-B-D-F-A♭
G7♯9♭5	1-3-♭5-♭7-♯9	G-B-D♭-F-A♯
G7♭9♭5	1-3-♭5-♭7-♭9	G-B-D♭-F-A♭
G7♯9♯5	1-3-♯5-♭7-♯9	G-B-D♯-F-A♯
G7♭9♯5	1-3-♯5-♭7-♭9	G-B-D♯-F-A♭
G7♯11	1-3-5-♭7-♯11	G-B-D-F-C♯

DOMINANT SEVENTH, SHARP FIFTH ARPEGGIOS

The same sweeping rule applies to these forms as to the previously learned forms. If there are two notes on a string, the first note is picked, and the second note is played with a hammer-on if ascending, or a pull-off if descending. If there are three notes on a string, the first note is picked, the second note is sounded with a slide, and the third is articulated with a hammer-on (ascending) or a pull-off (descending).

Here are four arpeggio forms for G7♯5 (G–B–D♯–F).

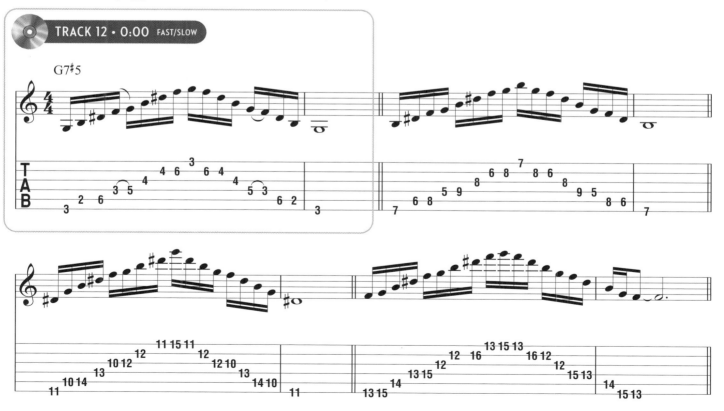

33

DOMINANT SEVENTH, FLAT FIFTH ARPEGGIOS

Here are four arpeggio forms for G7♭5 (G–B–D♭–F). Notice that there are several open-string notes in the root-position form. Pick-hand muting is key here for clear-sounding arpeggios.

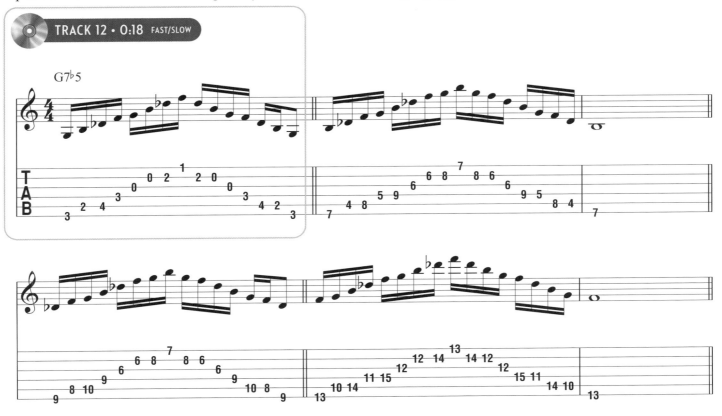

MORE ALTERED ARPEGGIOS

The following section contains arpeggio forms for G7♯9, G7♭9, G7♭5♭9, G7♯5♭9, G7♯5♯9, G7♭5♯9, and G7♯11 chords. For these shapes, I have included picking instructions between the staves, as the sweeping rules mentioned in previous sections do not always apply to these forms.

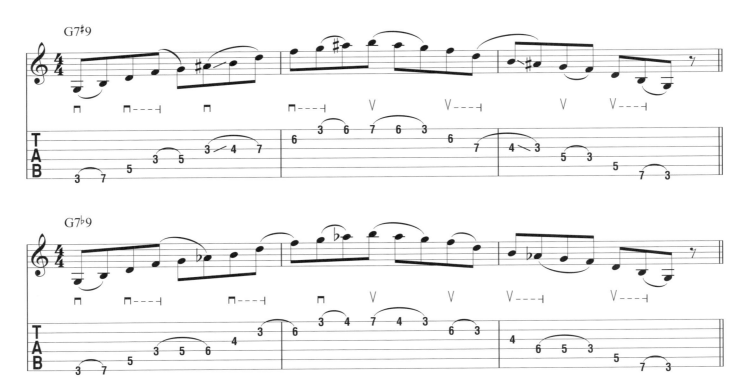

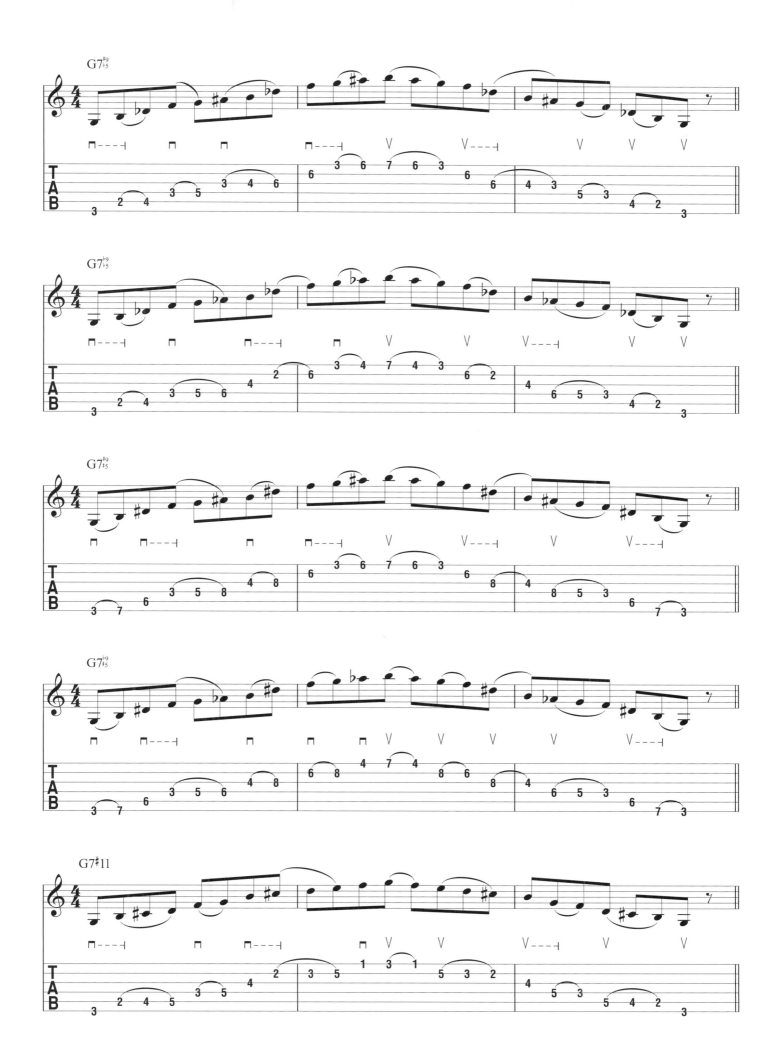

CHAPTER 5
OCTAVE ARPEGGIOS

Octave arpeggios are shapes that span three octaves, each having the exact same form. To create octave arpeggios, we stack three two-string octave shapes on string sets 6–5, 4–3, and 2–1. Because of the repetition found in octave shapes, playing a three-octave arpeggio is not much different than playing a one octave arpeggio. These arpeggios are linear in nature and can help you break out of "position playing" during your solos.

All of the arpeggios in this section are based on a G root note and should be played in all keys.

TRIAD ARPEGGIOS

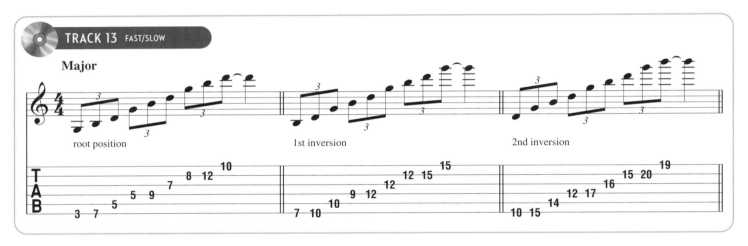

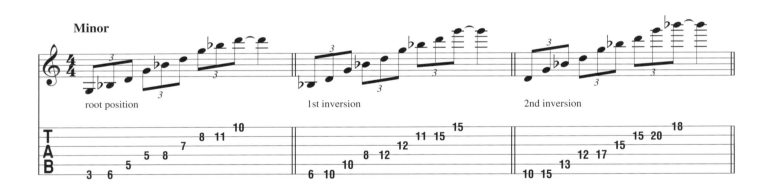

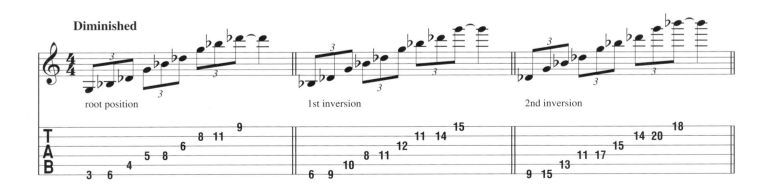

Augmented

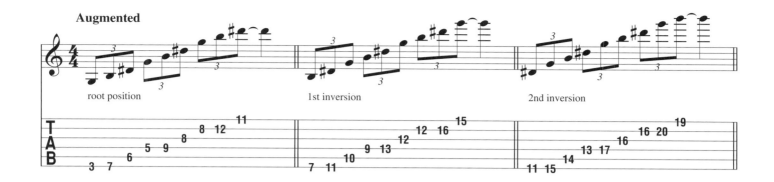

SEVENTH ARPEGGIOS

The following section contains octave arpeggio forms for various seventh-chord tonalities.

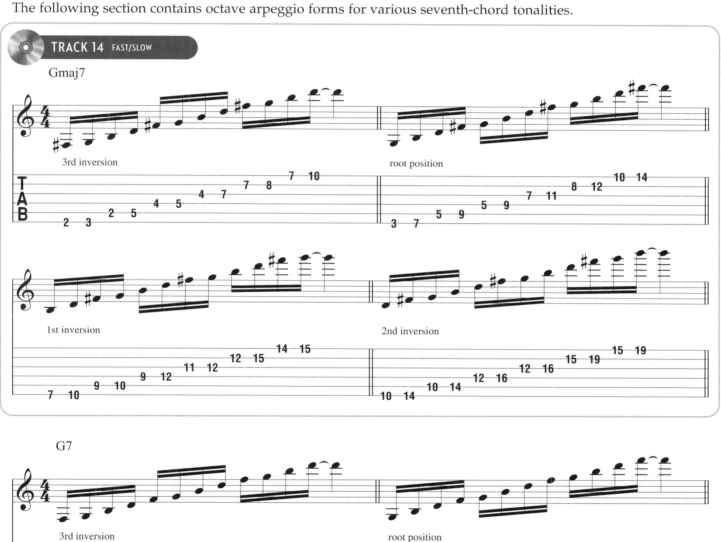

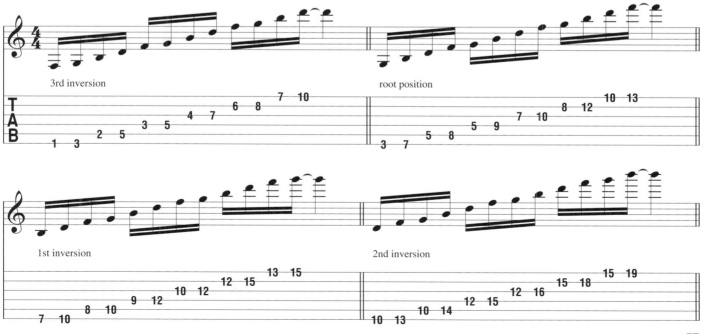

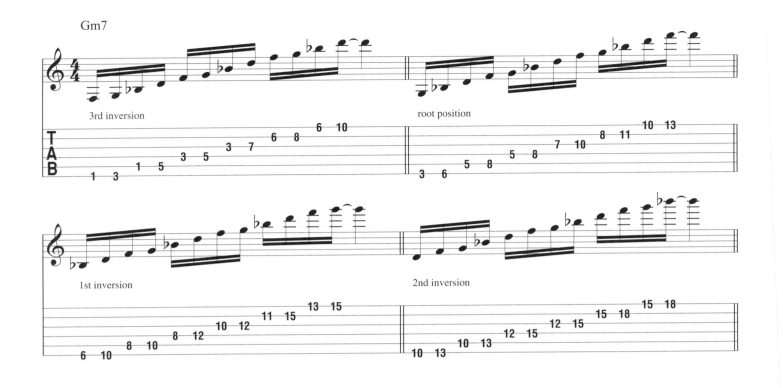

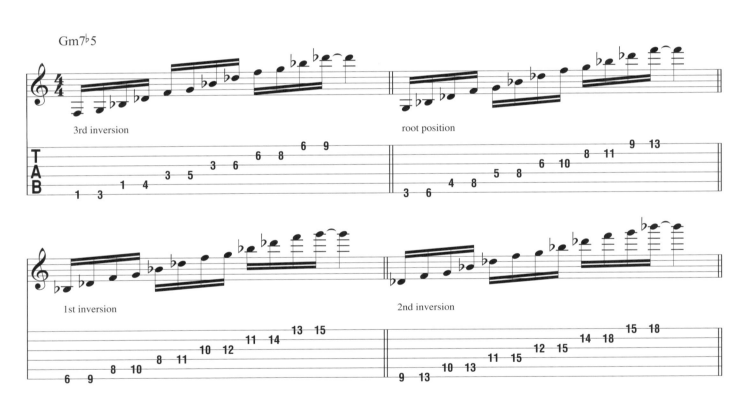

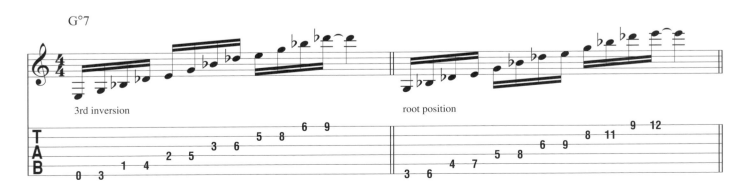

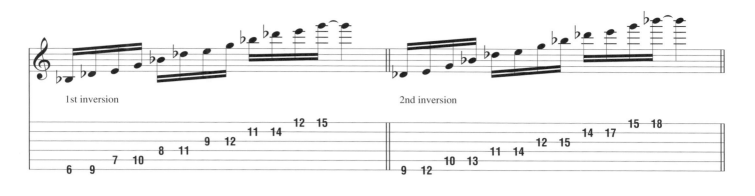

1st inversion

2nd inversion

Gmaj7♯11

3rd inversion

root position

1st inversion

2nd inversion

G7♭5

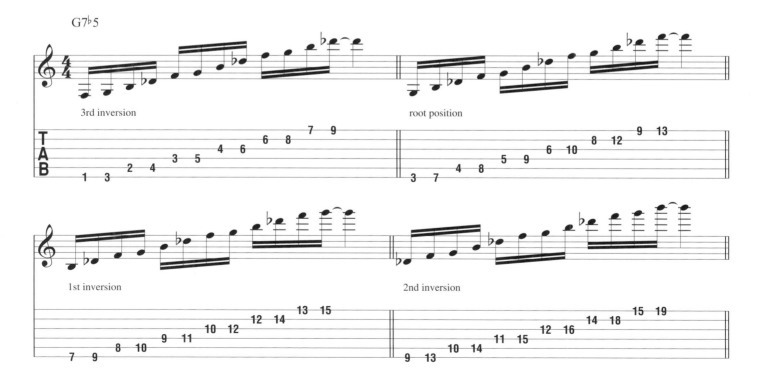

3rd inversion

root position

1st inversion

2nd inversion

ARPEGGIO FRAMING

Playing arpeggios alone in your solos will get boring in a hurry. To remedy this, try adding scale tones to your octave arpeggios, for extra color. I call this concept *arpeggio framing*, where your lines comprise notes from a given mode, framed by the notes of the appropriate arpeggio.

Here are several examples of scales framed with their associated arpeggios.

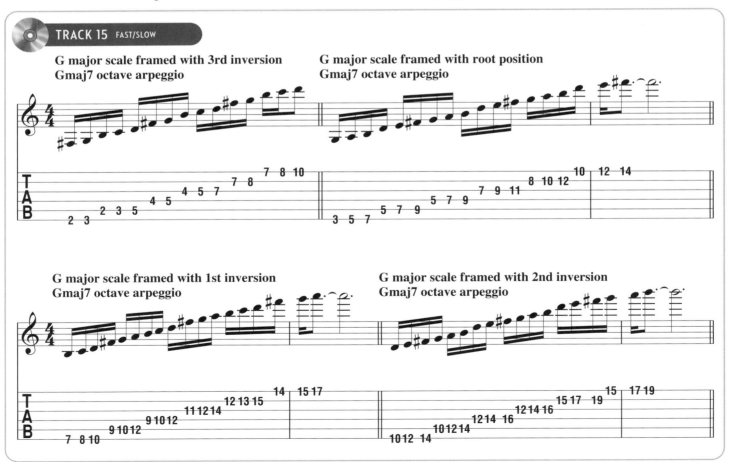

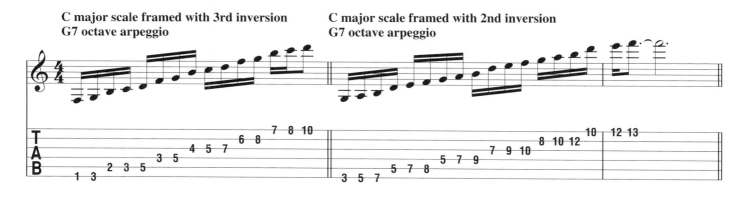

**C major scale framed with 3rd inversion
G7 octave arpeggio**

**C major scale framed with 2nd inversion
G7 octave arpeggio**

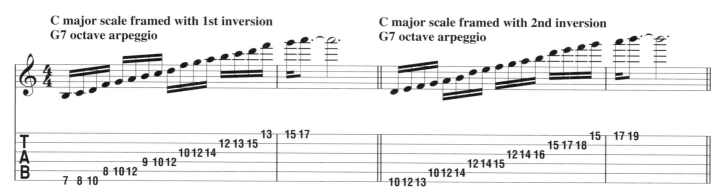

**C major scale framed with 1st inversion
G7 octave arpeggio**

**C major scale framed with 2nd inversion
G7 octave arpeggio**

As you practice the framing arpeggio approach, keep this noteworthy point in mind. For the Gmaj7 arpeggio, we framed a G major scale, of course. But there was another choice. The Gmaj7 chord is not only found in the key of G but also in the key of D. Thus, we can also frame the D major scale with the Gmaj7 chord. You can do so by raising all the C notes to C♯ in the Gmaj7 example.

You can do the same with the minor seventh chords, as every key has three minor seventh chords in it. For example, using a Gm7 arpeggio, you can frame F major (G Dorian), E♭ major (G Phrygian), and B♭ major (G Aeolian) scales.

OCTAVE ARPEGGIO PATTERNS

To give your octave arpeggios a little more energy, try using sequenced patterns such as the ones in the following section. Here we demonstrate ascending patterns for the root-position Gmaj7, G7, Gm7, Gm7♭5, G°7, and G7♯5 arpeggios. You can play these with either strict alternate picking, or with hammer-ons and pull-offs (as shown in the first two examples).

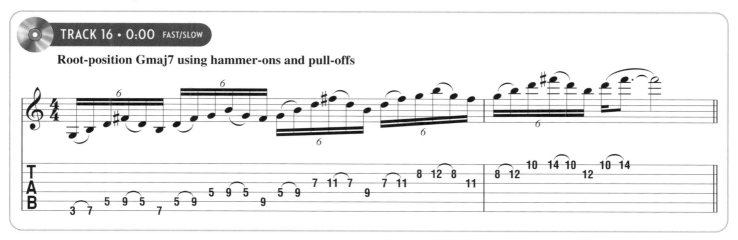

TRACK 16 · 0:00 FAST/SLOW

Root-position Gmaj7 using hammer-ons and pull-offs

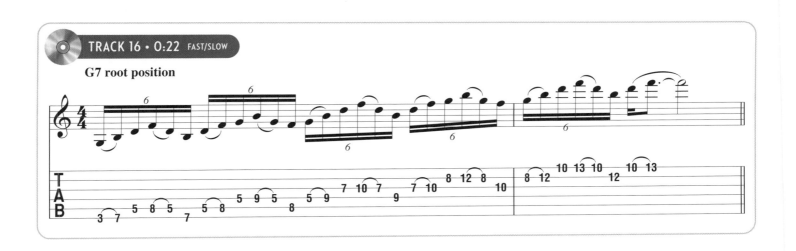

G7 root position

Gm7 root position

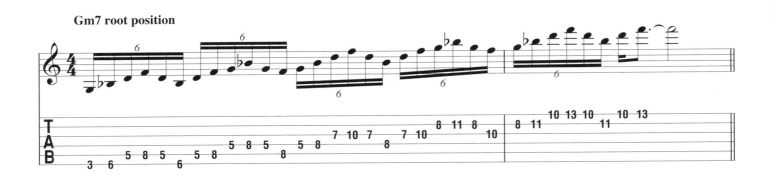

Gm7♭5 root position

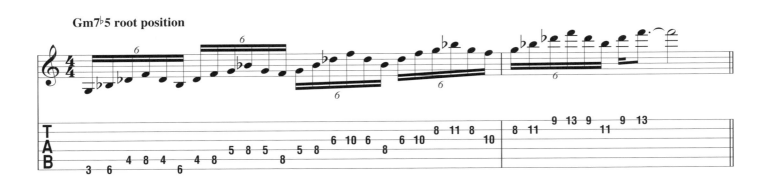

G°7 root position

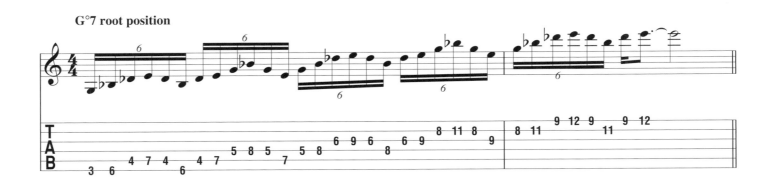

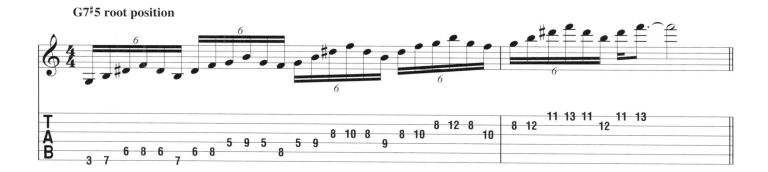

G7#5 root position

DESCENDING FORMS

To get the descending forms of the preceding patterns, simply play the tablature backwards. The Gmaj7 root position example is notated here.

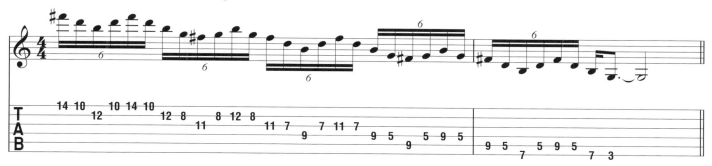

Gmaj7 root position (descending)

Try practicing these examples by ascending one inversion and then descending the next higher inversion. For example, after ascending the Gmaj7 root-position form above, you would descend the Gmaj7 1st-inversion form.

CHAPTER 6
TAPPING ARPEGGIOS

The term *tapping* refers to using one or more fingers on your picking hand on the fretboard to execute notes in the arpeggio. This technique can produce very smooth legato arpeggio sounds as well as enable wide intervallic jumps. Eddie Van Halen was one of the first players to make tapping an integral part of his guitar style. Since he made the technique popular, guitarists such as Nuno Bettencourt, Reb Beach, and Jeff Watson, as well as jazzer Stanley Jordan, have brought tapping to an even higher level by using several or even all four fingers of the picking hand to execute passages.

BASIC TAPPING

Probably the most basic example of tapping arpeggios is adding an extra note on the top string to a triad arpeggio form. Here is a G major root triad arpeggio to demonstrate the technique.

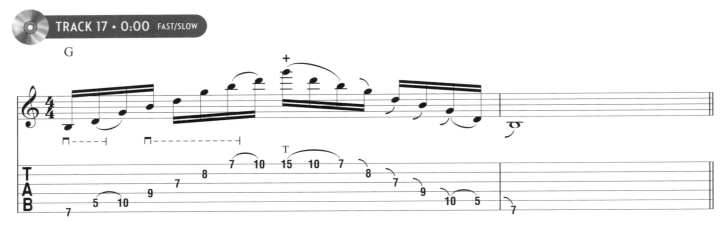

The example above is shown with a tap at the fifteenth fret, adding a G note on the high E string, three octaves away. In theory, any note could have been tapped with the right hand—the fourteenth fret would add the major 7th (F♯) to the G major triad, whereas the twelfth fret would add a 6th (E) to the major triad.

Notice also that the descending part of the arpeggio uses nothing but hammer-ons and pull-offs. Arpeggio forms that have notes crossing over to adjacent strings at different frets make this legato style of descending arpeggios much easier. Still, you'll need to use enough fret-hand force to sound these "hammer-ons from nowhere" at a volume equal to the sweep-picked notes of the ascent.

Here is a similar example using a Gmaj13 form from Chapter 3.

This next example demonstrates a descending arpeggio phrase in the key of C major using taps with hammer-ons and pull-offs.

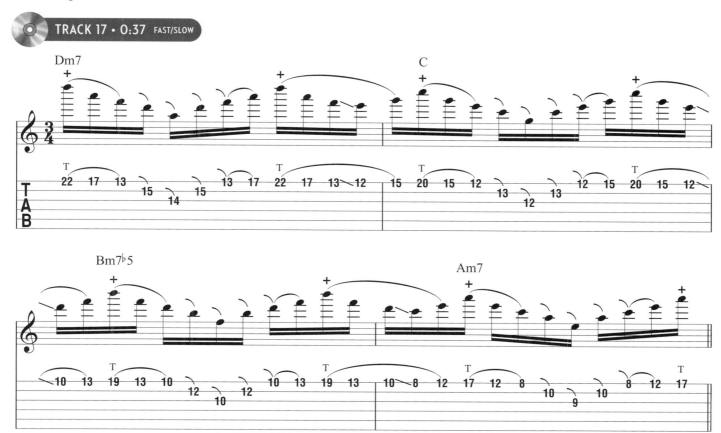

CROSS TAPPING

When playing arpeggio-based tapping phrases, you're not limited to tapping only on the top string. You can also use the *cross tapping* technique, in which you tap notes on several strings within the arpeggio. Here is a descending arpeggio phrase in A major to demonstrate the concept. Note the two position shifts that require you to use your pinky finger to fret a note previously fretted with your index finger.

This next example, based on a D7 arpeggio, uses cross tapping in conjunction with string skipping.

TAPPING ON EVERY STRING

Tapping on every string requires hammering onto every note below the tap on the ascent, and pulling off every note below the tap on the descent. Arpeggio runs that require a tapped note on every string can be viewed as stacking arpeggios in two parts: the left hand and the right hand. Many times the left- and right-hand parts are built from triad arpeggios stacked on top of each other. For example, the left hand part may play a root-position G major arpeggio starting on the fifth string, while the right hand taps out a first-inversion G major arpeggio starting on that same string.

Stacking different triads can also create extended arpeggios. For example, if the left hand plays a root-position G major form starting on the fifth string, and the right hand taps out a root-position B minor form on that same string, they combine to create a Gmaj7 arpeggio. This is very similar to how extended chords were constructed in Chapter 3.

If you're having trouble getting the following arpeggios under your fingers, try isolating the tapping part from the left-hand part and practice them separately. Isolating the parts will also stimulate new ideas for how to use this technique.

Triad Arpeggio Stacking

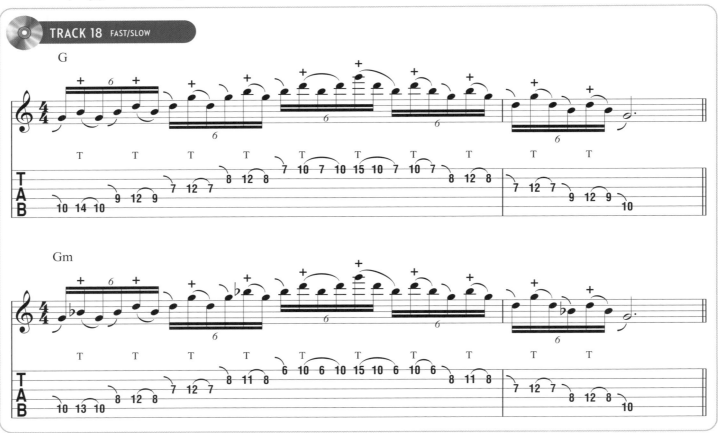

Gmaj7

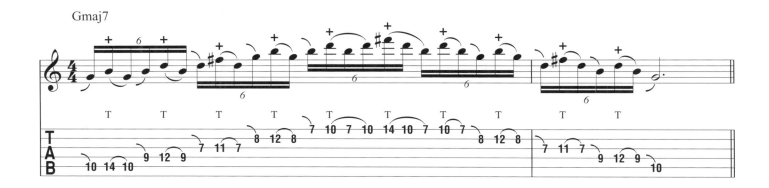

G7

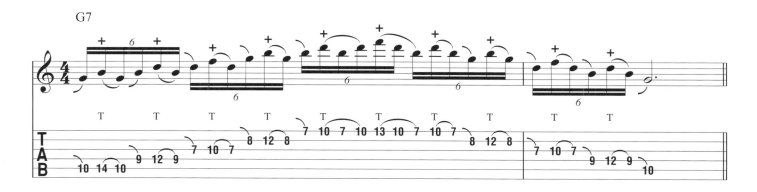

Gm7

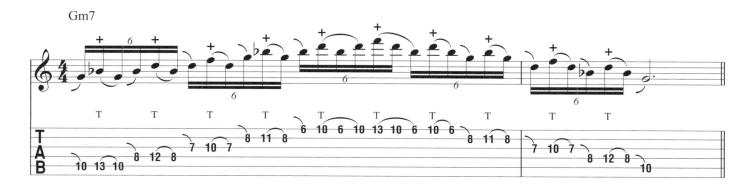

G7♭5♭9 (Stacked Tritones)

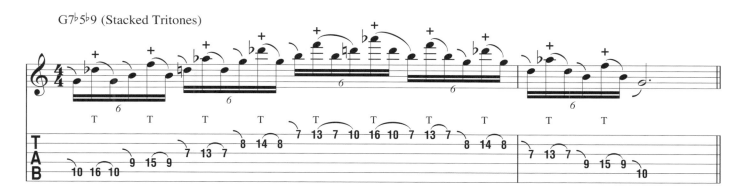

Gmaj9

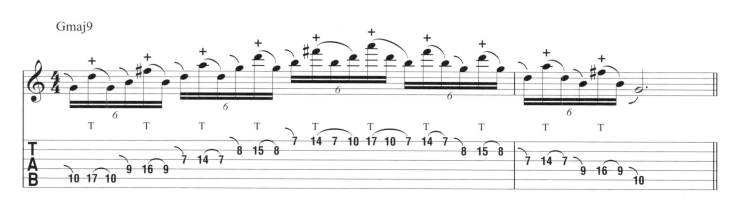

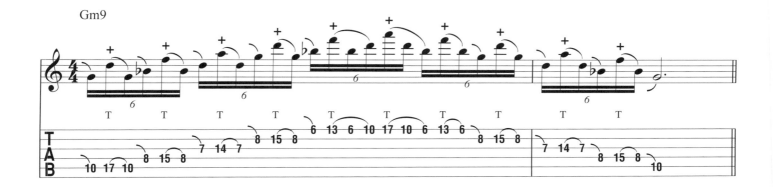

Gm9

Octave Arpeggio Stacking

Similar to the stacked triads approach, when playing stacked octave arpeggios, the left hand plays an octave arpeggio form, while the right hand taps the next-higher octave arpeggio inversion. These patterns are more difficult to play than the previous stacked triad tapping forms, but with practice, they eventually will become manageable.

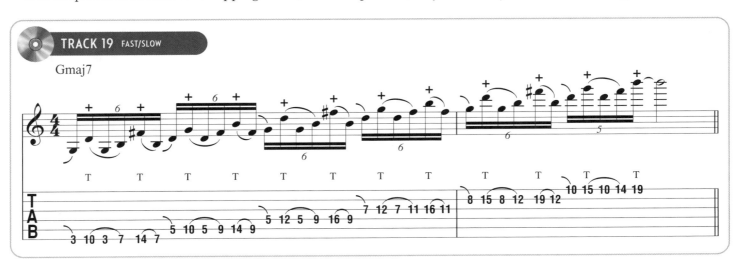

TRACK 19 FAST/SLOW

Gmaj7

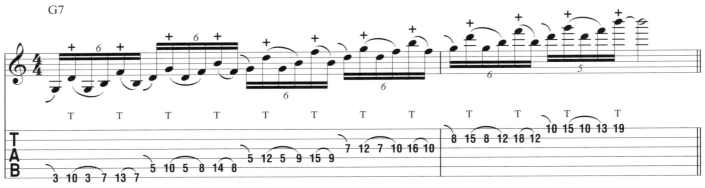

G7

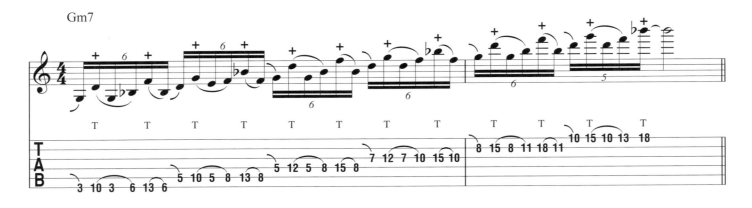

Gm7

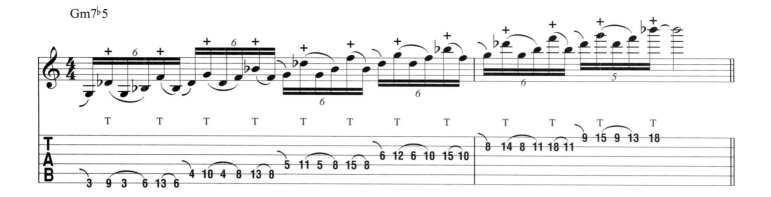

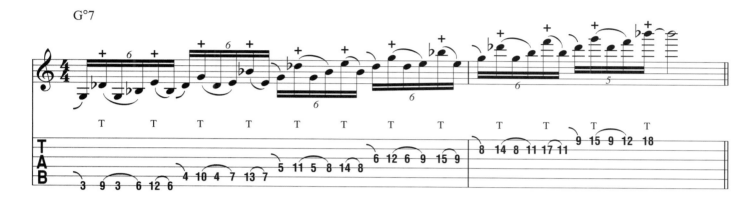

MULTI-STRING TAPPING

No lesson on tapping would be complete if it did not include a few words about using multiple fingers of the right hand. The next example demonstrates how this technique can be used to create truly pianistic sounds. Notice that when you isolate the left and right hand parts, each is based on diatonic 5th intervals. Understanding this pattern will make its execution a little easier. Use the index and ring fingers of the right hand for the taps. This technique may require a damper, such as a sock or a cotton ponytail holder, to be placed around the neck at the nut, to eliminate extraneous string noise.

TRACK 20 FAST/SLOW

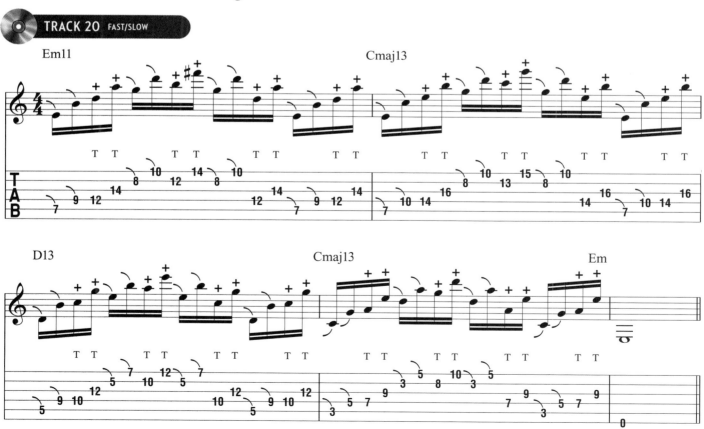

CHAPTER 7
ARPEGGIOS AND STRING SKIPPING

Thus far, we've focused on arpeggio forms that lay out across all six strings of the guitar, but it's possible—and sometimes advantageous—to organize the notes so they fall only on some of the strings. When you do this, you'll need to use the *string skipping* technique.

To see how these arpeggio forms lie on the fretboard, here are three C major arpeggio forms.

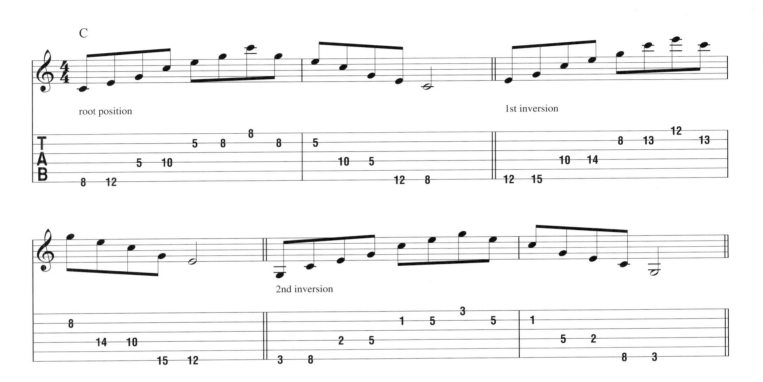

You will notice that there are some pretty big stretches and position jumps in these forms, thus making them a little uncomfortable to play using traditional fretting and picking methods. I have found that utilizing the *two-hand tapping* technique not only makes them easier to execute but also can create some pretty interesting sounds. Here is root-position C major arpeggio, with the higher note on each string performed with a right-hand fingertap. The ascending portion of the arpeggio is exactly the same as the version without using two-hand tapping, however, the descending portion changes to allow the left hand to initiate the first note on every string.

TRACK 21 FAST/SLOW

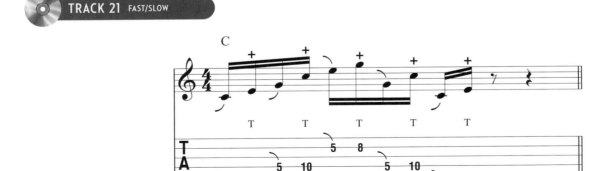

Notice that the stretches are not an issue when using two-hand tapping. Experiment with this technique on some of the other forms and tonalities.

We can build on this idea a bit more by backtracking after each string-skip. This results in an arpeggio sequence that covers all six of the strings instead of just three. Essentially, this approach involves stacking two triad arpeggios, similar to what we did in the previous chapter on two-hand tapping, only using string-skipping.

Here is an example using the root-position G major arpeggio for the left hand part and the first-inversion G major arpeggio for the right-hand tapping part.

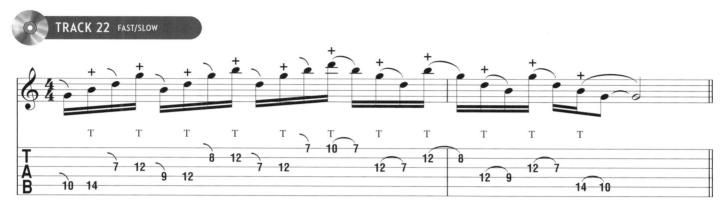

Two-hand tapping also presents the easiest way to play seventh arpeggios in string-skipping forms. To avoid the need to hammer on all of the notes, the ascent up the arpeggio form is not a strict one. For example, here is a root-position Cmaj7 arpeggio form.

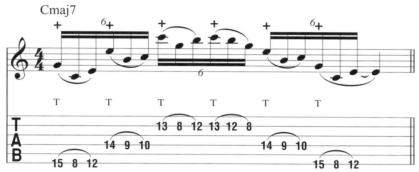

OCTAVE DISPLACEMENT

As stated earlier, playing basic arpeggio forms up and down can get boring in a hurry. To add some interesting sounds to very simple note sequences, try using *octave displacement*.

The obvious way to ascend a C major arpeggio in two octaves would be to play straight up the note sequence C–E–G–C–E–G, from low to high. However, there is no rule stating that you must play it in that order. Instead, you might start on the low C, and then play the E from the next higher octave, returning to the lower octave to play the G, and so on. Here are a few examples of this approach, using a C major arpeggio.

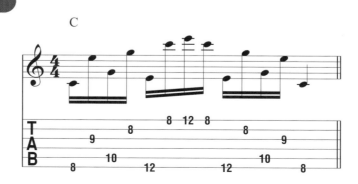

51

In this next example, we displace the octave on the 5th degree (G) of the arpeggio, for a different sound.

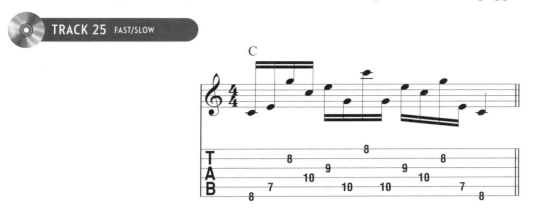

STRING SKIPPING WITH MULTI-STRING TAPPING

Now, let's use some octave displacement in the context of string-skipping arpeggio forms executed with two-hand tapping. To do this, however, you will need to tap more than one note per string with your right hand. In each of the following arpeggio phrases, your right hand's index and ring fingers to play the tapped notes.

The first example outlines a Dmaj7 arpeggio. The first two notes (D–F#) are executed with the index and pinky fingers of the left hand, the next three notes (A–C#–A) with the index and ring fingers of the right hand, and so on. You can clearly see how difficult it would be to execute this run using only one hand, as the wide intervallic jumps make it next to impossible to play in a conventional manner.

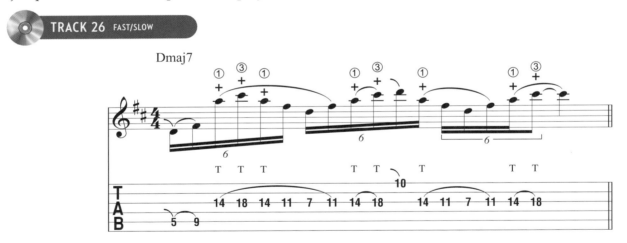

This Am11 arpeggio form uses the same technique as the Dmaj7 arpeggio above.

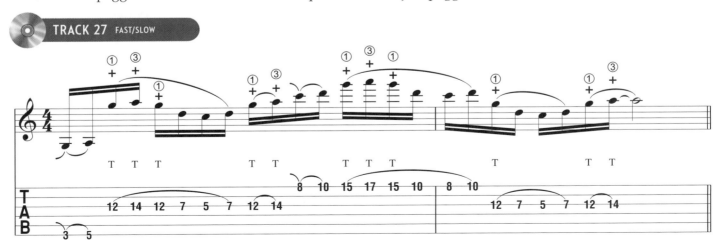

CHAPTER 8
KEY TRANSPOSITION

Learning to play the arpeggios presented in this book is not easy. They require advanced techniques and a whole lot of patience and determination along the way. And it would be a shame if you put in all that time to master these forms up to tempo but then were unable to reproduce them when your singer says he needs you to play in a different key.

Throughout this book, I've reminded you to practice the arpeggio forms and phrases in all keys, because you never know when you'll be called on to play in an unfamiliar key. In this chapter, we'll focus on making those transpositions a little easier.

CYCLE OF 5THS

One of the most useful tools for learning key transposition is the *cycle of 5ths*. It is commonly depicted as a circular arrangement of all 12 notes of the chromatic scale, each a 5th above the preceding one when moving clockwise through the cycle, or a 4th above when moving counterclockwise through it.

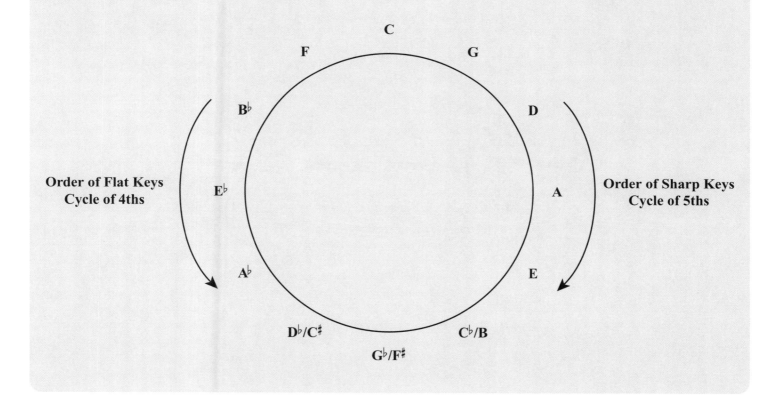

To demonstrate key transposition, we'll play through the cycle using three-string major-triad arpeggios. Be sure to apply this same procedure to minor, diminished, and augmented forms as well.

To start, let's find the C major arpeggio closest to the nut, which is the second-inversion form, starting on the open G note on the third string. Next in the cycle of 5ths is G major, so we need to find the G major arpeggio closest to open position, play that, and so on.

Here is the entire cycle of 5ths in major triad arpeggio forms, with each in as close to open position as possible.

Another useful way to practice key transposition is to play the arpeggios found within the harmonized major scale, working your way all the way through the cycle of 5ths. The following examples show how to apply this idea using three-string triad arpeggios.

Key of C

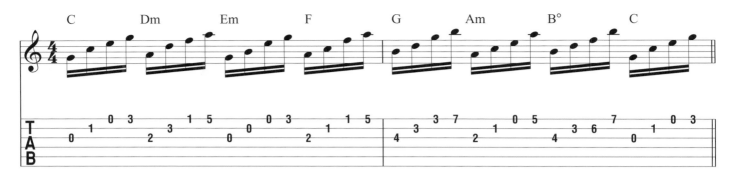

Key of G

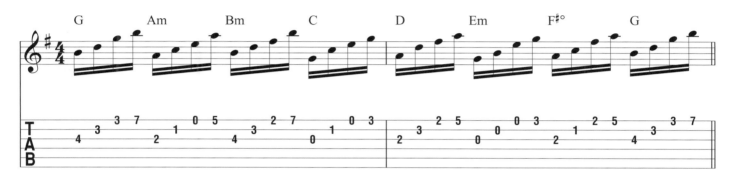

Key of D

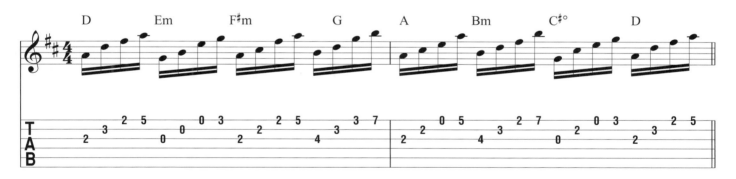

Key of A

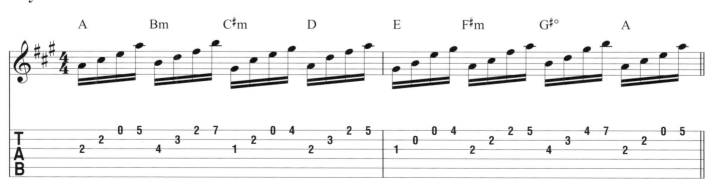

Key of E

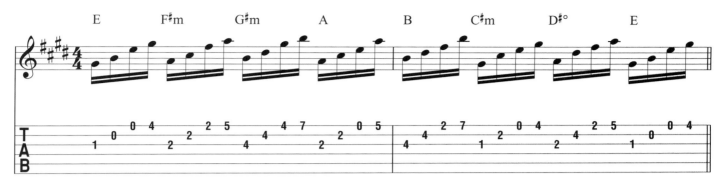

Key of B

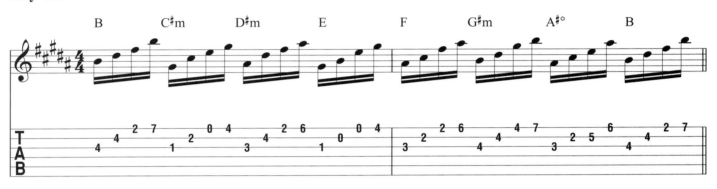

Key of F

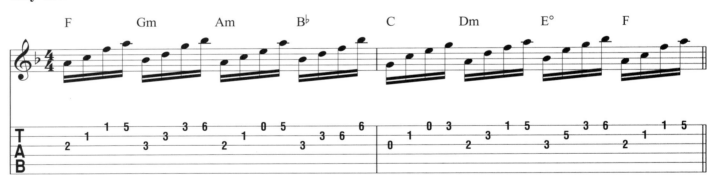

Key of B♭

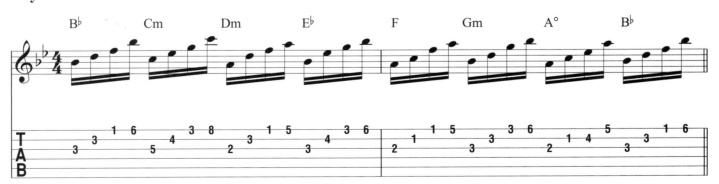

Key of E♭

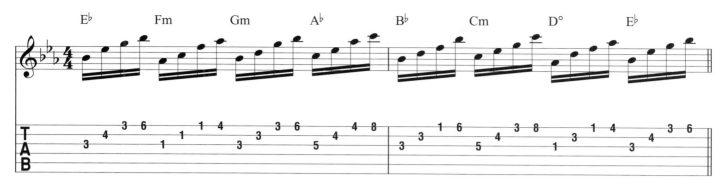

Key of A♭

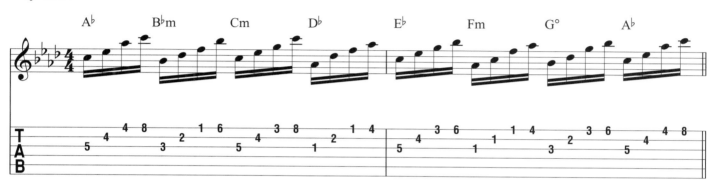

Key of D♭

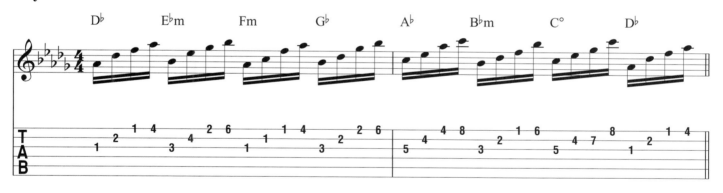

Key of G♭

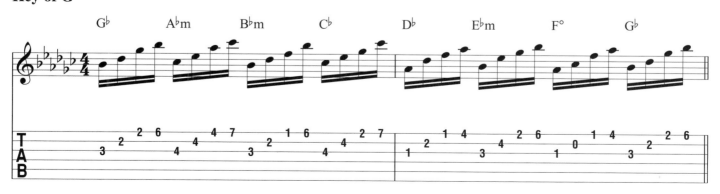

SIX-STRING MAJOR SEVENTH ARPEGGIOS

Now, let's take the exercise up a notch, playing major seventh arpeggios through the cycle of 5ths, as close to the nut as possible. After you've played through this exercise, try it with dominant, minor, and diminished seventh arpeggios, too.

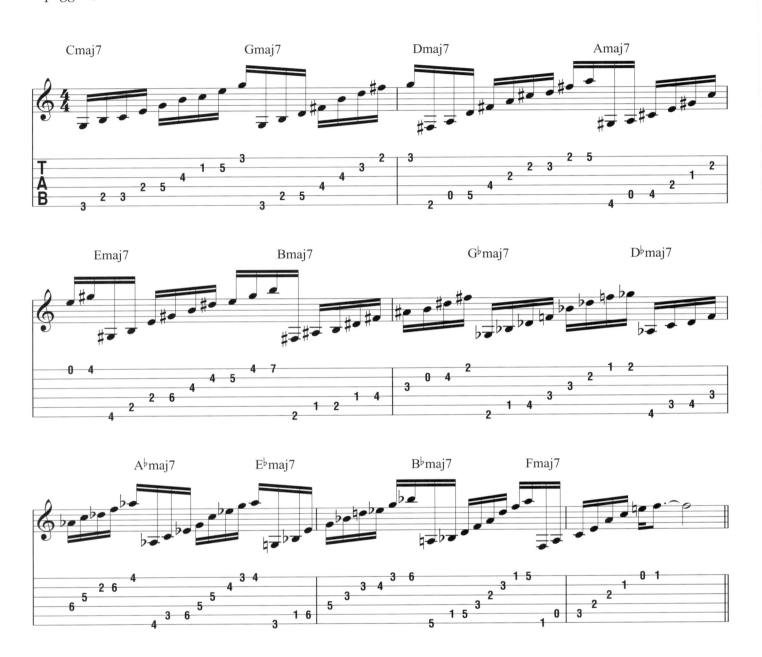

The examples in this section were given using three-string triad arpeggios and six-string major seventh arpeggios. As you practice playing arpeggios in all keys, be sure to play four- and five-string forms as well as all the different chord qualities (minor, dominant, diminished, and so on). Further, be sure to play these various forms in several positions on the fretboard.

CHAPTER 9
ARPEGGIO EXAMPLES

Sometimes all the words in the world cannot get a point across as well as an example. The examples in this chapter are designed to illustrate many of the ways that you can use arpeggios to construct interesting lines and patterns. Use these licks and phrases as a stimulus for creating your own new and original ideas. And, as always, be sure to practice them in all keys.

This A Mixolydian phrase will work well over any A dominant chord.

This example is based on the root-position Gmaj13 arpeggio shape and combines sweep picking with legato lines.

Here, an upper-octave Gmaj13 arpeggio gets the legato treatment along with some tapping and position-shifting with the pinky.

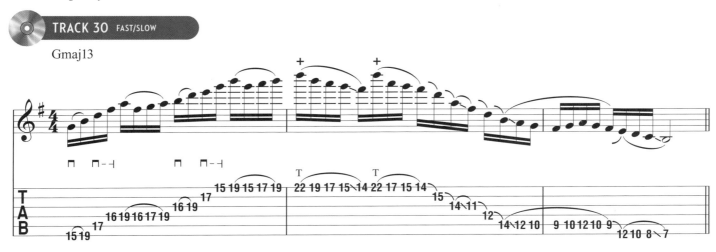

Here's another G major arpeggio phrase combining sweep picking, tapping, and position shifts.

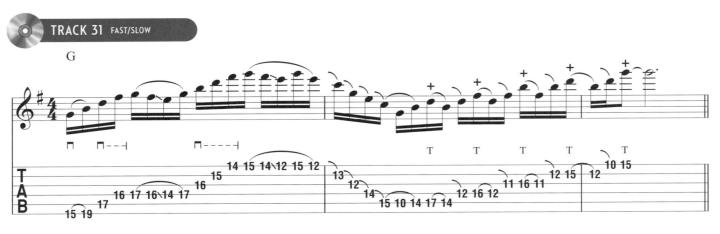

Here, several G major arpeggio forms are connected to cover most of the fretboard.

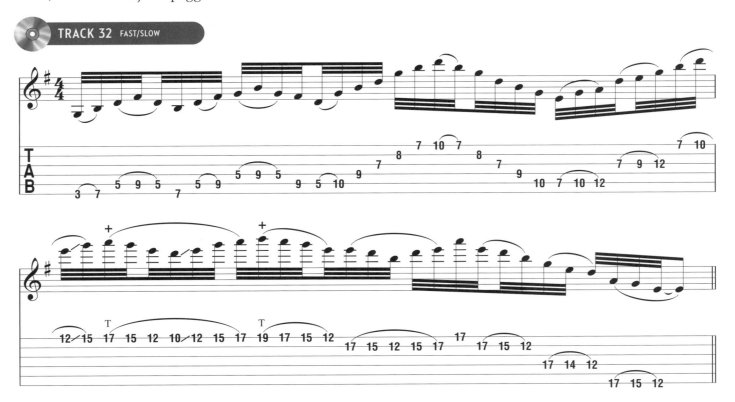

The following Cmaj9 run uses second-inversion Cmaj7 and Gmaj7 octave arpeggios.

This example, in the key of G, connects several diatonic triad arpeggios together for a variation on Pachelbel's "Canon."

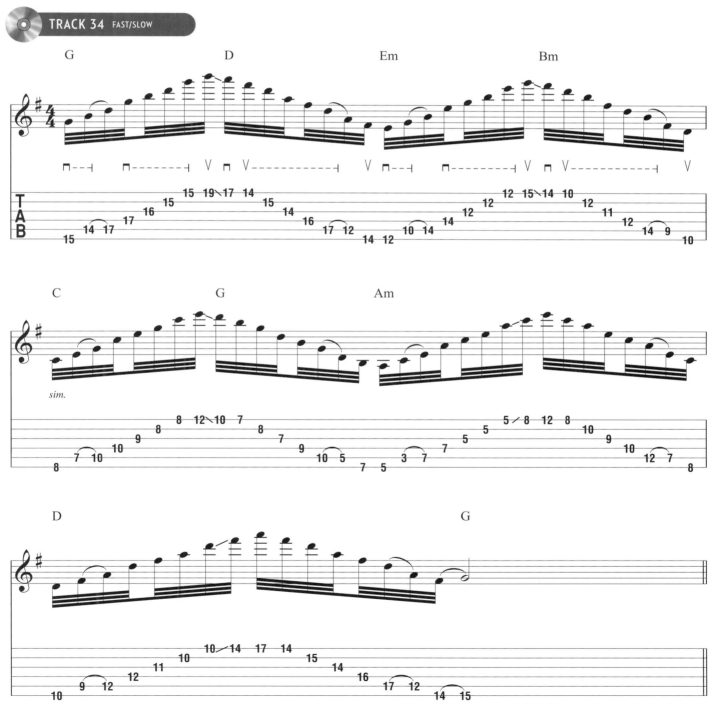

Our final example illustrates a B minor triad arpeggio combined with a second-inversion Dmaj7 octave arpeggio, with added tapped notes.

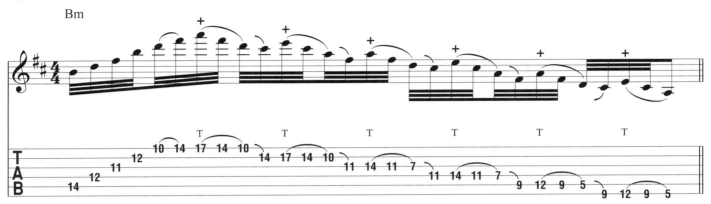

Guitar Notation Legend

Guitar music can be notated three different ways: on a *musical staff*, in *tablature*, and in *rhythm slashes*.

RHYTHM SLASHES are written above the staff. Strum chords in the rhythm indicated. Use the chord diagrams found at the top of the first page of the transcription for the appropriate chord voicings. Round noteheads indicate single notes.

THE MUSICAL STAFF shows pitches and rhythms and is divided by bar lines into measures. Pitches are named after the first seven letters of the alphabet.

TABLATURE graphically represents the guitar fingerboard. Each horizontal line represents a string, and each number represents a fret.

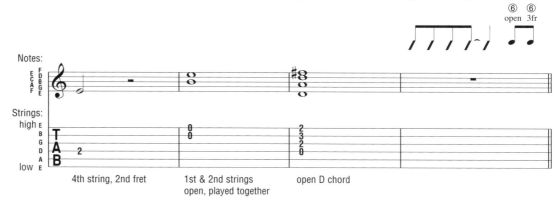

Definitions for Special Guitar Notation

HALF-STEP BEND: Strike the note and bend up 1/2 step.

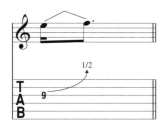

WHOLE-STEP BEND: Strike the note and bend up one step.

GRACE NOTE BEND: Strike the note and immediately bend up as indicated.

SLIGHT (MICROTONE) BEND: Strike the note and bend up 1/4 step.

BEND AND RELEASE: Strike the note and bend up as indicated, then release back to the original note. Only the first note is struck.

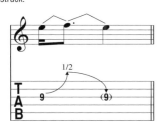

PRE-BEND: Bend the note as indicated, then strike it.

PRE-BEND AND RELEASE: Bend the note as indicated. Strike it and release the bend back to the original note.

UNISON BEND: Strike the two notes simultaneously and bend the lower note up to the pitch of the higher.

VIBRATO: The string is vibrated by rapidly bending and releasing the note with the fretting hand.

WIDE VIBRATO: The pitch is varied to a greater degree by vibrating with the fretting hand.

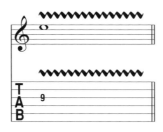

HAMMER-ON: Strike the first (lower) note with one finger, then sound the higher note (on the same string) with another finger by fretting it without picking.

PULL-OFF: Place both fingers on the notes to be sounded. Strike the first note and without picking, pull the finger off to sound the second (lower) note.

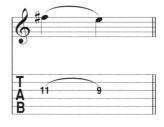

LEGATO SLIDE: Strike the first note and then slide the same fret-hand finger up or down to the second note. The second note is not struck.

SHIFT SLIDE: Same as legato slide, except the second note is struck.

TRILL: Very rapidly alternate between the notes indicated by continuously hammering on and pulling off.

TAPPING: Hammer ("tap") the fret indicated with the pick-hand index or middle finger and pull off to the note fretted by the fret hand.

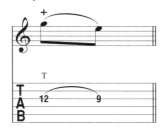

NATURAL HARMONIC: Strike the note while the fret-hand lightly touches the string directly over the fret indicated.

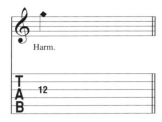

PINCH HARMONIC: The note is fretted normally and a harmonic is produced by adding the edge of the thumb or the tip of the index finger of the pick hand to the normal pick attack.

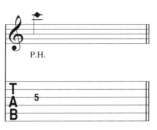

HARP HARMONIC: The note is fretted normally and a harmonic is produced by gently resting the pick hand's index finger directly above the indicated fret (in parentheses) while the pick hand's thumb or pick assists by plucking the appropriate string.

PICK SCRAPE: The edge of the pick is rubbed down (or up) the string, producing a scratchy sound.

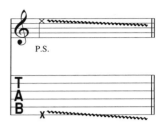

MUFFLED STRINGS: A percussive sound is produced by laying the fret hand across the string(s) without depressing, and striking them with the pick hand.

PALM MUTING: The note is partially muted by the pick hand lightly touching the string(s) just before the bridge.

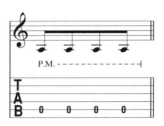

RAKE: Drag the pick across the strings indicated with a single motion.

TREMOLO PICKING: The note is picked as rapidly and continuously as possible.

ARPEGGIATE: Play the notes of the chord indicated by quickly rolling them from bottom to top.

VIBRATO BAR DIVE AND RETURN: The pitch of the note or chord is dropped a specified number of steps (in rhythm), then returned to the original pitch.

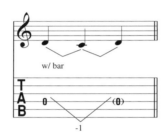

VIBRATO BAR SCOOP: Depress the bar just before striking the note, then quickly release the bar.

VIBRATO BAR DIP: Strike the note and then immediately drop a specified number of steps, then release back to the original pitch.

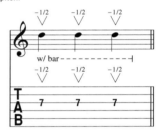

Additional Musical Definitions

 *(accent)* • Accentuate note (play it louder).

(accent) • Accentuate note with great intensity.

(staccato) • Play the note short.

 • Downstroke

V • Upstroke

D.S. al Coda • Go back to the sign (𝄋), then play until the measure marked "*To Coda*," then skip to the section labelled "**Coda**."

D.C. al Fine • Go back to the beginning of the song and play until the measure marked "***Fine***" (end).

Rhy. Fig. • Label used to recall a recurring accompaniment pattern (usually chordal).

Riff • Label used to recall composed, melodic lines (usually single notes) which recur.

Fill • Label used to identify a brief melodic figure which is to be inserted into the arrangement.

Rhy. Fill • A chordal version of a Fill.

tacet • Instrument is silent (drops out).

 • Repeat measures between signs.

• When a repeated section has different endings, play the first ending only the first time and the second ending only the second time.

NOTE: Tablature numbers in parentheses mean:
1. The note is being sustained over a system (note in standard notation is tied), or
2. The note is sustained, but a new articulation (such as a hammer-on, pull-off, slide or vibrato) begins, or
3. The note is a barely audible "ghost" note (note in standard notation is also in parentheses).